this & Object Prototypes

Kyle Simpson

Beijing · Cambridge · Farnham · Köln · Sebastopol · Tokyo

this & Object Prototypes

by Kyle Simpson

Printed in the United States of America.

Published by O'Reilly Media, Inc., 1005 Gravenstein Highway North, Sebastopol, CA 95472.

O'Reilly books may be purchased for educational, business, or sales promotional use. Online editions are also available for most titles (*http://my.safaribooksonline.com*). For more information, contact our corporate/institutional sales department: 800-998-9938 or *corporate@oreilly.com*.

Editors: Simon St. Laurent and Brian MacDonald	**Proofreader:** Linley Dolby
	Cover Designer: Karen Montgomery
Production Editor: Kristen Brown	**Interior Designer:** David Futato
Copyeditor: Charles Roumeliotis	**Illustrator:** Rebecca Demarest

July 2014:   First Edition

Revision History for the First Edition:

2014-07-09:   First release

See *http://oreilly.com/catalog/errata.csp?isbn=9781491904152* for release details.

ISBN: 978-1-491-90415-2

[LSI]

Table of Contents

Foreword

While reading this book in preparation for writing this foreword, I was forced to reflect on how I learned JavaScript and how much it has changed over the last 15 years that I have been programming and developing with it.

When I started using JavaScript 15 years ago, the practice of using non-HTML technologies such as CSS and JS in your web pages was called DHTML or Dynamic HTML. Back then, the usefulness of JavaScript varied greatly and seemed to be tilted toward adding animated snowflakes to your web pages or dynamic clocks that told the time in the status bar. Suffice it to say, I didn't really pay much attention to JavaScript in the early part of my career because of the novelty of the implementations that I often found on the Internet.

It wasn't until 2005 that I first rediscovered JavaScript as a real programming language that I needed to pay closer attention to. After digging into the first beta release of Google Maps, I was hooked on the potential it had. At the time, Google Maps was a first-of-its-kind application—it allowed you to move a map around with your mouse, zoom in and out, and make server requests without reloading the page —all with JavaScript. It seemed like magic!

When anything seems like magic, it is usually a good indication that you are at the dawn of a new way of doing things. And boy, was I not wrong—fast-forwarding to today, I would say that JavaScript is one of the primary languages I use for both client- and server-side programming, and I wouldn't have it any other way.

One of my regrets as I look over the past 15 years is that I didn't give JavaScript more of a chance before 2005, or more accurately, that I lacked the foresight to see JavaScript as a true programming language that is just as useful as C++, C#, Java, and many others.

If I had this *You Don't Know JS* series of books at the start of my career, my career history would look much different than it does today. And that is one of the things I love about this series: it explains JavaScript at a level that builds your understanding as you go through the series, but in a fun and informative way.

this & Object Prototypes is a wonderful continuation to the series. It does a great and natural job of building on the prior book, *Scope & Closures*, and extending that knowledge to a very important part of the JS language, the this keyword and prototypes. These two simple things are pivotal for what you will learn in the future books, because they are foundational to doing real programming with JavaScript. The concept of how to create objects, relate them, and extend them to represent things in your application is necessary to create large and complex applications in JavaScript. And without them, creating complex applications (such as Google Maps) wouldn't be possible in JavaScript.

I would say that the vast majority of web developers probably have never built a JavaScript object and just treat the language as event-binding glue between buttons and AJAX requests. I was in that camp at a point in my career, but after I learned how to master prototypes and create objects in JavaScript, a world of possibilities opened up for me. If you fall into the category of just creating event-binding glue code, this book is a must-read; if you just need a refresher, this book will be a go-to resource for you. Either way, you will not be disappointed. Trust me!

—Nick Berardi
nickberardi.com, @nberardi

Preface

I'm sure you noticed, but "JS" in the book series title is not an abbreviation for words used to curse about JavaScript, though cursing at the language's quirks is something we can probably all identify with!

From the earliest days of the Web, JavaScript has been a foundational technology that drives interactive experience around the content we consume. While flickering mouse trails and annoying pop-up prompts may be where JavaScript started, nearly two decades later, the technology and capability of JavaScript has grown many orders of magnitude, and few doubt its importance at the heart of the world's most widely available software platform: the Web.

But as a language, it has perpetually been a target for a great deal of criticism, owing partly to its heritage but even more to its design philosophy. Even the name evokes, as Brendan Eich once put it, "dumb kid brother" status next to its more mature older brother Java. But the name is merely an accident of politics and marketing. The two languages are vastly different in many important ways. "JavaScript" is as related to "Java" as "Carnival" is to "Car."

Because JavaScript borrows concepts and syntax idioms from several languages, including proud C-style procedural roots as well as subtle, less obvious Scheme/Lisp-style functional roots, it is exceedingly approachable to a broad audience of developers, even those with little to no programming experience. The "Hello World" of JavaScript is so simple that the language is inviting and easy to get comfortable with in early exposure.

While JavaScript is perhaps one of the easiest languages to get up and running with, its eccentricities make solid mastery of the language a vastly less common occurrence than in many other languages. Where it takes a pretty in-depth knowledge of a language like C or C++ to write a full-scale program, full-scale production JavaScript can, and often does, barely scratch the surface of what the language can do.

Sophisticated concepts that are deeply rooted into the language tend instead to surface themselves in *seemingly* simplistic ways, such as passing around functions as callbacks, which encourages the JavaScript developer to just use the language as-is and not worry too much about what's going on under the hood.

It is simultaneously a simple, easy-to-use language that has broad appeal, and a complex and nuanced collection of language mechanics that without careful study will elude *true understanding* even for the most seasoned of JavaScript developers.

Therein lies the paradox of JavaScript, the Achilles' heel of the language, the challenge we are presently addressing. Because JavaScript *can* be used without understanding, the understanding of the language is often never attained.

Mission

If at every point that you encounter a surprise or frustration in JavaScript, your response is to add it to the blacklist (as some are accustomed to doing), you soon will be relegated to a hollow shell of the richness of JavaScript.

While this subset has been famously dubbed "The Good Parts," I would implore you, dear reader, to instead consider it the "The Easy Parts," "The Safe Parts," or even "The Incomplete Parts."

This *You Don't Know JS* book series offers a contrary challenge: learn and deeply understand *all* of JavaScript, even and especially "The Tough Parts."

Here, we address head-on the tendency of JS developers to learn "just enough" to get by, without ever forcing themselves to learn exactly how and why the language behaves the way it does. Furthermore, we eschew the common advice to retreat when the road gets rough.

I am not content, nor should you be, at stopping once something just works and not really knowing *why*. I gently challenge you to journey down that bumpy "road less traveled" and embrace all that JavaScript is and can do. With that knowledge, no technique, no framework, no popular buzzword acronym of the week will be beyond your understanding.

These books each take on specific core parts of the language that are most commonly misunderstood or under-understood, and dive very deep and exhaustively into them. You should come away from reading with a firm confidence in your understanding, not just of the theoretical, but the practical "what you need to know" bits.

The JavaScript you know right now is probably parts handed down to you by others who've been burned by incomplete understanding. *That* JavaScript is but a shadow of the true language. You don't really know JavaScript, *yet*, but if you dig into this series, you will. Read on, my friends. JavaScript awaits you.

Review

JavaScript is awesome. It's easy to learn partially, and much harder to learn completely (or even *sufficiently*). When developers encounter confusion, they usually blame the language instead of their lack of understanding. These books aim to fix that, inspiring a strong appreciation for the language you can now, and *should*, deeply know.

 Many of the examples in this book assume modern (and future-reaching) JavaScript engine environments, such as ES6. Some code may not work as described if run in older (pre-ES6) engines.

Conventions Used in This Book

The following typographical conventions are used in this book:

Italic
> Indicates new terms, URLs, email addresses, filenames, and file extensions.

`Constant width`
> Used for program listings, as well as within paragraphs to refer to program elements such as variable or function names, databases, data types, environment variables, statements, and keywords.

Constant width bold
> Shows commands or other text that should be typed literally by the user.

Constant width italic
> Shows text that should be replaced with user-supplied values or by values determined by context.

 This element signifies a tip or suggestion.

 This element signifies a general note.

 This element indicates a warning or caution.

Using Code Examples

Supplemental material (code examples, exercises, etc.) is available for download at *http://bit.ly/ydkjs-this-code*.

This book is here to help you get your job done. In general, if example code is offered with this book, you may use it in your programs and documentation. You do not need to contact us for permission unless you're reproducing a significant portion of the code. For example, writing a program that uses several chunks of code from this book does not require permission. Selling or distributing a CD-ROM of examples from O'Reilly books does require permission. Answering a question by citing this book and quoting example code does not require permission. Incorporating a significant amount of example code from this book into your product's documentation does require permission.

We appreciate, but do not require, attribution. An attribution usually includes the title, author, publisher, and ISBN. For example: *"this & Object Prototypes* by Kyle Simpson (O'Reilly). Copyright 2014 Getify Solutions, Inc., 978-1-491-90415-2."

If you feel your use of code examples falls outside fair use or the permission given above, feel free to contact us at *permissions@oreilly.com*.

Safari® Books Online

 Safari Books Online is an on-demand digital library that delivers expert content in both book and video form from the world's leading authors in technology and business.

Technology professionals, software developers, web designers, and business and creative professionals use Safari Books Online as their primary resource for research, problem solving, learning, and certification training.

Safari Books Online offers a range of product mixes and pricing programs for organizations, government agencies, and individuals. Subscribers have access to thousands of books, training videos, and prepublication manuscripts in one fully searchable database from publishers like O'Reilly Media, Prentice Hall Professional, Addison-Wesley Professional, Microsoft Press, Sams, Que, Peachpit Press, Focal Press, Cisco Press, John Wiley & Sons, Syngress, Morgan Kaufmann, IBM Redbooks, Packt, Adobe Press, FT Press, Apress, Manning, New Riders, McGraw-Hill, Jones & Bartlett, Course Technology, and dozens more. For more information about Safari Books Online, please visit us online.

How to Contact Us

Please address comments and questions concerning this book to the publisher:

O'Reilly Media, Inc.
1005 Gravenstein Highway North
Sebastopol, CA 95472
800-998-9938 (in the United States or Canada)
707-829-0515 (international or local)
707-829-0104 (fax)

We have a web page for this book, where we list errata, examples, and any additional information. You can access this page at *http://bit.ly/ ydk-js-this-object-prototypes*.

To comment or ask technical questions about this book, send email to *bookquestions@oreilly.com*.

For more information about our books, courses, conferences, and news, see our website at *http://www.oreilly.com*.

Find us on Facebook: *http://facebook.com/oreilly*

Follow us on Twitter: *http://twitter.com/oreillymedia*

Watch us on YouTube: *http://www.youtube.com/oreillymedia*

Check out the full *You Don't Know JS* series: *http://YouDont KnowJS.com*

this or That?

One of the most confused mechanisms in JavaScript is the this keyword. It's a special identifier keyword that's automatically defined in the scope of every function, but what exactly it refers to bedevils even seasoned JavaScript developers.

> Any sufficiently *advanced* technology is indistinguishable from magic.
>
> — Arthur C. Clarke

JavaScript's this mechanism isn't actually *that* advanced, but developers often paraphrase that quote in their own mind by inserting "complex" or "confusing," and there's no question that without lack of clear understanding, this can seem downright magical in *your* confusion.

 The word "this" is a terribly common pronoun in general discourse. So, it can be very difficult, especially verbally, to determine whether we are using "this" as a pronoun or using it to refer to the actual keyword identifier. For clarity, I will always use this to refer to the special keyword, and "this" or *this* or this otherwise.

Why this?

If the this mechanism is so confusing, even to seasoned JavaScript developers, one may wonder why it's even useful. Is it more trouble than it's worth? Before we jump into the *how*, we should examine the *why*.

Let's try to illustrate the motivation and utility of this:

```
function identify() {
    return this.name.toUpperCase();
}

function speak() {
    var greeting = "Hello, I'm " + identify.call( this );
    console.log( greeting );
}

var me = {
    name: "Kyle"
};

var you = {
    name: "Reader"
};

identify.call( me ); // KYLE
identify.call( you ); // READER

speak.call( me ); // Hello, I'm KYLE
speak.call( you ); // Hello, I'm READER
```

If the *how* of this snippet confuses you, don't worry! We'll get to that shortly. Just set those questions aside briefly so we can look into the *why* more clearly.

This code snippet allows the identify() and speak() functions to be reused against multiple *context* objects (me and you), rather than needing a separate version of the function for each object.

Instead of relying on this, you could have explicitly passed in a context object to both identify() and speak():

```
function identify(context) {
    return context.name.toUpperCase();
}

function speak(context) {
    var greeting = "Hello, I'm " + identify( context );
    console.log( greeting );
}

identify( you ); // READER
speak( me ); // Hello, I'm KYLE
```

However, the this mechanism provides a more elegant way of implicitly "passing along" an object reference, leading to cleaner API design and easier reuse.

The more complex your usage pattern is, the more clearly you'll see that passing context around as an explicit parameter is often messier than passing around a this context. When we explore objects and prototypes, you will see the helpfulness of a collection of functions being able to automatically reference the proper context object.

Confusions

We'll soon begin to explain how this actually works, but first we must dispel some misconceptions about how it *doesn't* actually work.

The name "this" creates confusion when developers try to think about it too literally. There are two meanings often assumed, but both are incorrect.

Itself

The first common temptation is to assume this refers to the function itself. That's a reasonable grammatical inference, at least.

Why would you want to refer to a function from inside itself? The most common reasons would be things like recursion (calling a function from inside itself) or having an event handler that can unbind itself when it's first called.

Developers new to JavaScript's mechanisms often think that referencing the function as an object (all functions in JavaScript are objects!) lets you store *state* (values in properties) between function calls. While this is certainly possible and has some limited uses, the rest of the book will expound on many other patterns for *better* places to store state besides the function object.

But for just a moment, we'll explore that pattern, to illustrate how this doesn't let a function get a reference to itself like we might have assumed.

Consider the following code, where we attempt to track how many times a function (foo) was called:

```
function foo(num) {
    console.log( "foo: " + num );

    // keep track of how many times `foo` is called
    this.count++;
}

foo.count = 0;

var i;

for (i=0; i<10; i++) {
    if (i > 5) {
        foo( i );
    }
}
// foo: 6
// foo: 7
// foo: 8
// foo: 9

// how many times was `foo` called?
console.log( foo.count ); // 0 -- WTF?
```

foo.count is *still* 0, even though the four console.log statements clearly indicate foo(..) was in fact called four times. The frustration stems from a *too literal* interpretation of what this (in this.count++) means.

When the code executes foo.count = 0, indeed it's adding a property count to the function object foo. But for the this.count reference inside of the function, this is not in fact pointing *at all* to that function object, and so even though the property names are the same, the root objects are different, and confusion ensues.

 A responsible developer *should* ask at this point, "If I was in-crementing a count property but it wasn't the one I expected, which count *was* I incrementing?" In fact, were she to dig deeper, she would find that she had accidentally created a global variable count (see Chapter 2 for *how* that happened!), and it currently has the value NaN. Of course, once she identi-fies this peculiar outcome, she then has a whole other set of questions: "How was it global, and why did it end up NaN in-stead of some proper count value?" (see Chapter 2).

Instead of stopping at this point and digging into why the this reference doesn't seem to be behaving as expected, and answering those tough but important questions, many developers simply avoid the issue altogether, and hack toward some other solution, such as creating another object to hold the count property:

```
function foo(num) {
    console.log( "foo: " + num );

    // keep track of how many times `foo` is called
    data.count++;
}

var data = {
    count: 0
};

var i;

for (i=0; i<10; i++) {
    if (i > 5) {
        foo( i );
    }
}
// foo: 6
// foo: 7
// foo: 8
// foo: 9

// how many times was `foo` called?
console.log( data.count ); // 4
```

While it is true that this approach "solves" the problem, unfortunately it simply ignores the real problem—lack of understanding what this means and how it works—and instead falls back to the comfort zone of a more familiar mechanism: lexical scope.

Lexical scope is a perfectly fine and useful mechanism; I am not belittling the use of it, by any means (see the *Scope & Closures* title of this book series). But constantly guessing at how to use this, and usually being wrong, is not a good reason to retreat back to lexical scope and never learn why this eludes you.

To reference a function object from inside itself, this by itself will typically be insufficient. You generally need a reference to the function object via a lexical identifier (variable) that points at it.

Consider these two functions:

```
function foo() {
    foo.count = 4; // `foo` refers to itself
}

setTimeout( function(){
    // anonymous function (no name), cannot
    // refer to itself
}, 10 );
```

In the first function, called a "named function," foo is a reference that can be used to refer to the function from inside itself.

But in the second example, the function callback passed to setTime out(..) has no name identifier (called an "anonymous function"), so there's no proper way to refer to the function object itself.

 The old-school but now deprecated and frowned-upon argu ments.callee reference inside a function *also* points to the function object of the currently executing function. This ref erence is typically the only way to access an anonymous func tion's object from inside itself. The best approach, however, is to avoid the use of anonymous functions altogether, at least for those that require a self-reference, and instead use a named function (expression). arguments.callee is deprecated and should not be used.

So another solution to our running example would have been to use the foo identifier as a function object reference in each place, and not use this at all, which works:

```
function foo(num) {
    console.log( "foo: " + num );

    // keep track of how many times `foo` is called
    foo.count++;
}

foo.count = 0;

var i;

for (i=0; i<10; i++) {
    if (i > 5) {
        foo( i );
    }
}
```

```
// foo: 6
// foo: 7
// foo: 8
// foo: 9

// how many times was `foo` called?
console.log( foo.count ); // 4
```

However, that approach similarly side-steps *actual* understanding of this and relies entirely on the lexical scoping of variable foo.

Yet another way of approaching the issue is to force this to actually point at the foo function object:

```
function foo(num) {
    console.log( "foo: " + num );

    // keep track of how many times `foo` is called
    // Note: `this` IS actually `foo` now, based on
    // how `foo` is called (see below)
    this.count++;
}

foo.count = 0;

var i;

for (i=0; i<10; i++) {
    if (i > 5) {
        // using `call(..)`, we ensure the `this`
        // points at the function object (`foo`) itself
        foo.call( foo, i );
    }
}
// foo: 6
// foo: 7
// foo: 8
// foo: 9

// how many times was `foo` called?
console.log( foo.count ); // 4
```

Instead of avoiding this, we embrace it. We'll explain in a little bit *how* such techniques work much more completely, so don't worry if you're still a bit confused!

Its Scope

The next most common misconception about the meaning of this is that it somehow refers to the function's scope. It's a tricky question, because in one sense there is some truth, but in the other sense, it's quite misguided.

To be clear, this does not, in any way, refer to a function's lexical scope. It is true that internally, scope is kind of like an object with properties for each of the available identifiers. But the scope "object" is not accessible to JavaScript code. It's an inner part of the *engine*'s implementation.

Consider code that attempts (and fails!) to cross over the boundary and use this to implicitly refer to a function's lexical scope:

```
function foo() {
    var a = 2;
    this.bar();
}

function bar() {
    console.log( this.a );
}

foo(); //ReferenceError: a is not defined
```

There's more than one mistake in this snippet. While it may seem contrived, the code you see is a distillation of actual real-world code that has been exchanged in public community help forums. It's a wonderful (if not sad) illustration of just how misguided this assumptions can be.

First, an attempt is made to reference the bar() function via this.bar(). It is almost certainly an accident that it works, but we'll explain the *how* of that shortly. The most natural way to have invoked bar() would have been to omit the leading this. and just make a lexical reference to the identifier.

However, the developer who writes such code is attempting to use this to create a bridge between the lexical scopes of foo() and bar(), so that bar() has access to the variable a in the inner scope of foo(). No such bridge is possible. You cannot use a this reference to look something up in a lexical scope. It is not possible.

Every time you feel yourself trying to mix lexical scope look-ups with this, remind yourself: *there is no bridge.*

What's this?

Having set aside various incorrect assumptions, let us now turn our attention to how the this mechanism really works.

We said earlier that this is not an author-time binding but a runtime binding. It is contextual based on the conditions of the function's invocation. this binding has nothing to do with where a function is declared, but has instead everything to do with the manner in which the function is called.

When a function is invoked, an activation record, otherwise known as an execution context, is created. This record contains information about where the function was called from (the call-stack), *how* the function was invoked, what parameters were passed, etc. One of the properties of this record is the this reference, which will be used for the duration of that function's execution.

In the next chapter, we will learn to find a function's call-site to determine how its execution will bind this.

Review

this binding is a constant source of confusion for the JavaScript developer who does not take the time to learn how the mechanism actually works. Guesses, trial and error, and blind copy and paste from Stack Overflow answers is not an effective or proper way to leverage *this* important this mechanism.

To learn this, you first have to learn what this is *not*, despite any assumptions or misconceptions that may lead you down those paths. this is neither a reference to the function itself, nor is it a reference to the function's *lexical* scope.

this is actually a binding that is made when a function is invoked, and *what* it references is determined entirely by the call-site where the function is called.

this All Makes Sense Now!

In Chapter 1, we discarded various misconceptions about this and learned instead that this is a binding made for each function invocation, based entirely on its call-site (how the function is called).

Call-Site

To understand this binding, we have to understand the *call-site*: the location in code where a function is called (not where it's declared). We must inspect the call-site to answer the question: what is *this* this a reference to?

Finding the call-site is generally "go locate where a function is called from," but it's not always that easy, as certain coding patterns can obscure the *true* call-site.

What's important is to think about the *call-stack* (the stack of functions that have been called to get us to the current moment in execution). The call-site we care about is *in* the invocation *before* the currently executing function.

Let's demonstrate the call-stack and call-site:

```
function baz() {
    // call-stack is: `baz`
    // so, our call-site is in the global scope

    console.log( "baz" );
    bar(); // <-- call-site for `bar`
}

function bar() {
```

```
        // call-stack is: `baz` -> `bar`
        // so, our call-site is in `baz`

        console.log( "bar" );
        foo(); // <-- call-site for `foo`
    }

    function foo() {
        // call-stack is: `baz` -> `bar` -> `foo`
        // so, our call-site is in `bar`

        console.log( "foo" );
    }

    baz(); // <-- call-site for `baz`
```

Take care when analyzing code to find the actual call-site (from the call-stack), because it's the only thing that matters for this binding.

 You can visualize a call-stack in your mind by looking at the chain of function calls in order, as we did with the comments in the previous snippet. But this is painstaking and error-prone. Another way of seeing the call-stack is using a debugger tool in your browser. Most modern desktop browsers have built-in developer tools that include a JS debugger. In the previous snippet, you could have set a breakpoint in the tools for the first line of the foo() function, or simply inserted the de bugger; statement on that first line. When you run the page, the debugger will pause at this location, and will show you a list of the functions that have been called to get to that line, which will be your call-stack. So, if you're trying to diagnose this binding, use the developer tools to get the call-stack, then find the second item from the top, and that will show you the real call-site.

Nothing but Rules

We turn our attention now to *how* the call-site determines where this will point during the execution of a function.

You must inspect the call-site and determine which of four rules applies. We will first explain each of these four rules independently, and then we will illustrate their order of precedence, if multiple rules *could* apply to the call-site.

Default Binding

The first rule we will examine comes from the most common case of function calls: standalone function invocation. Think of *this* this rule as the default catch-all rule when none of the other rules apply.

Consider the following code:

```
function foo() {
    console.log( this.a );
}

var a = 2;

foo(); // 2
```

The first thing to note, if you were not already aware, is that variables declared in the global scope, as var a = 2 is, are synonymous with global-object properties of the same name. They're not copies of each other, they *are* each other. Think of it as two sides of the same coin.

Second, we see that when foo() is called, this.a resolves to our global variable a. Why? Because in this case, the *default binding* for this applies to the function call, and so points this at the global object.

How do we know that the *default binding* rule applies here? We examine the call-site to see how foo() is called. In our snippet, foo() is called with a plain, undecorated function reference. None of the other rules we will demonstrate will apply here, so the *default binding* applies instead.

If strict mode is in effect, the global object is not eligible for the *default binding*, so the this is instead set to undefined:

```
function foo() {
    "use strict";

    console.log( this.a );
}

var a = 2;

foo(); // TypeError: `this` is `undefined`
```

A subtle but important detail is that though the overall this binding rules are entirely based on the call-site, the global object is only eligible for the *default binding* if the contents of foo() are not running in strict mode; the strict mode state of the call-site of foo() is irrelevant:

```
function foo() {
    console.log( this.a );
}

var a = 2;

(function(){
    "use strict";

    foo(); // 2
})();
```

 Intentionally mixing strict mode and non-strict mode together in your own code is generally frowned upon. Your entire program should probably either be strict or non-strict. However, sometimes you include a third-party library that has different strictness than your own code, so care must be taken over these subtle compatibility details.

Implicit Binding

Another rule to consider is whether the call-site has a context object, also referred to as an owning or containing object, though *these* alternate terms could be slightly misleading.

Consider:

```
function foo() {
    console.log( this.a );
}

var obj = {
    a: 2,
    foo: foo
};

obj.foo(); // 2
```

First, notice the manner in which foo() is declared and then later added as a reference property onto obj. Regardless of whether foo() is initially declared *on* foo, or is added as a reference later (as this snippet shows), in neither case is the function really "owned" or "contained" by the obj object.

However, the call-site *uses* the obj context to reference the function, so you *could* say that the obj object "owns" or "contains" the function reference at the time the function is called.

Whatever you choose to call this pattern, at the point that foo() is called, it's preceeded by an object reference to obj. When there is a context object for a function reference, the *implicit binding* rule says that it's *that* object that should be used for the function call's this binding. Because obj is the this for the foo() call, this.a is synonymous with obj.a.

Only the top/last level of an object property reference chain matters to the call-site. For instance:

```
function foo() {
    console.log( this.a );
}

var obj2 = {
    a: 42,
    foo: foo
};

var obj1 = {
    a: 2,
    obj2: obj2
};

obj1.obj2.foo(); // 42
```

Implicitly lost

One of the most common frustrations that this binding creates is when an *implicitly bound* function loses that binding, which usually means it falls back to the *default binding* of either the global object or undefined, depending on strict mode.

Consider:

```
function foo() {
    console.log( this.a );
}

var obj = {
    a: 2,
    foo: foo
};

var bar = obj.foo; // function reference/alias!
```

```
var a = "oops, global"; // `a` also property on global object

bar(); // "oops, global"
```

Even though bar appears to be a reference to obj.foo, in fact, it's really just another reference to foo itself. Moreover, the call-site is what matters, and the call-site is bar(), which is a plain, undecorated call, and thus the *default binding* applies.

The more subtle, more common, and more unexpected way this occurs is when we consider passing a callback function:

```
function foo() {
    console.log( this.a );
}

function doFoo(fn) {
    // `fn` is just another reference to `foo`

    fn(); // <-- call-site!
}

var obj = {
    a: 2,
    foo: foo
};

var a = "oops, global"; // `a` also property on global object

doFoo( obj.foo ); // "oops, global"
```

Parameter passing is just an implicit assignment, and since we're passing a function, it's an implicit reference assignment, so the end result is the same as the previous snippet.

What if the function you're passing your callback to is not your own, but built into the language? No difference, same outcome:

```
function foo() {
    console.log( this.a );
}

var obj = {
    a: 2,
    foo: foo
};

var a = "oops, global"; // `a` also property on global object

setTimeout( obj.foo, 100 ); // "oops, global"
```

Think about this crude theoretical pseudoimplementation of `setTi meout()` provided as a built-in from the JavaScript environment:

```
function setTimeout(fn,delay) {
    // wait (somehow) for `delay` milliseconds
    fn(); // <-- call-site!
}
```

It's quite common that our function callbacks *lose* their `this` binding, as we've just seen. But another way that `this` can surprise us is when the function we've passed our callback to intentionally changes the `this` for the call. Event handlers in popular JavaScript libraries are quite fond of forcing your callback to have a `this` that points to, for instance, the DOM element that triggered the event. While that may sometimes be useful, other times it can be downright infuriating. Unfortunately, these tools rarely let you choose.

Either way the `this` is changed unexpectedly, you are not really in control of how your callback function reference will be executed, so you have no way (yet) of controlling the call-site to give your intended binding. We'll see shortly a way of "fixing" that problem by *fixing* the `this`.

Explicit Binding

With *implicit binding*, as we just saw, we had to mutate the object in question to include a reference on itself to the function, and use this property function reference to indirectly (implicitly) bind `this` to the object.

But, what if you want to force a function call to use a particular object for the `this` binding, without putting a property function reference on the object?

"All" functions in the language have some utilities available to them (via their `[[Prototype]]`—more on that later), which can be useful for this task. Specifically, functions have `call(..)` and `apply(..)` methods. Technically, JavaScript host environments sometimes provide functions that are special enough (a kind way of putting it!) that they do not have such functionality. But those are few. The vast majority of functions provided, and certainly all functions you will create, do have access to `call(..)` and `apply(..)`.

How do these utilities work? They both take, as their first parameter, an object to use for the `this`, and then invoke the function with that this specified. Since you are directly stating what you want the `this` to be, we call it *explicit binding*.

Consider:

```
function foo() {
    console.log( this.a );
}

var obj = {
    a: 2
};

foo.call( obj ); // 2
```

Invoking `foo` with *explicit binding* by `foo.call(..)` allows us to force its `this` to be `obj`.

If you pass a simple primitive value (of type `string`, `boolean`, or `num ber`) as the `this` binding, the primitive value is wrapped in its object-form (`new String(..)`, `new Boolean(..)`, or `new Number(..)`, respectively). This is often referred to as "boxing."

 With respect to `this` binding, `call(..)` and `apply(..)` are identical. They *do* behave differently with their additional parameters, but that's not something we care about presently.

Unfortunately, *explicit binding* alone still doesn't offer any solution to the issue mentioned previously, of a function "losing" its intended `this` binding, or just having it paved over by a framework, etc.

Hard binding

But a variation pattern around *explicit binding* actually does the trick. Consider:

```
function foo() {
    console.log( this.a );
}

var obj = {
    a: 2
};

var bar = function() {
    foo.call( obj );
```

```
};

bar(); // 2
setTimeout( bar, 100 ); // 2

// hard-bound `bar` can no longer have its `this` overridden
bar.call( window ); // 2
```

Let's examine how this variation works. We create a function bar()
which, internally, manually calls foo.call(obj), thereby forcibly invoking foo with obj binding for this. No matter how you later invoke
the function bar, it will always manually invoke foo with obj. This
binding is both explicit and strong, so we call it *hard binding*.

The most typical way to wrap a function with a *hard binding* creates a
pass-through of any arguments passed and any return value received:

```
function foo(something) {
    console.log( this.a, something );
    return this.a + something;
}

var obj = {
    a: 2
};

var bar = function() {
    return foo.apply( obj, arguments );
};

var b = bar( 3 ); // 2 3
console.log( b ); // 5
```

Another way to express this pattern is to create a reusable helper:

```
function foo(something) {
    console.log( this.a, something );
    return this.a + something;
}

// simple `bind` helper
function bind(fn, obj) {
    return function() {
        return fn.apply( obj, arguments );
    };
}

var obj = {
    a: 2
};
```

```
var bar = bind( foo, obj );

var b = bar( 3 ); // 2 3
console.log( b ); // 5
```

Since *hard binding* is such a common pattern, it's provided with a built-in utility as of ES5, `Function.prototype.bind`, and it's used like this:

```
function foo(something) {
    console.log( this.a, something );
    return this.a + something;
}

var obj = {
    a: 2
};

var bar = foo.bind( obj );

var b = bar( 3 ); // 2 3
console.log( b ); // 5
```

`bind(..)` returns a new function that is hardcoded to call the original function with the `this` context set as you specified.

API call "contexts"

Many libraries' functions, and indeed many new built-in functions in the JavaScript language and host environment, provide an optional parameter, usually called "context," which is designed as a work-around for you not having to use `bind(..)` to ensure your callback function uses a particular `this`.

For instance:

```
function foo(el) {
    console.log( el, this.id );
}

var obj = {
    id: "awesome"
};

// use `obj` as `this` for `foo(..)` calls
[1, 2, 3].forEach( foo, obj );
// 1 awesome  2 awesome  3 awesome
```

Internally, these various functions almost certainly use *explicit binding* via `call(..)` or `apply(..)`, saving you the trouble.

new Binding

The fourth and final rule for this binding requires us to rethink a very common misconception about functions and objects in JavaScript.

In traditional class-oriented languages, "constructors" are special methods attached to classes, and when the class is instantiated with a new operator, the constructor of that class is called. This usually looks something like:

```
something = new MyClass(..);
```

JavaScript has a new operator, and the code pattern to use it looks basically identical to what we see in those class-oriented languages; most developers assume that JavaScript's mechanism is doing something similar. However, there really is *no connection* to class-oriented functionality implied by new usage in JS.

First, let's redefine what a "constructor" in JavaScript is. In JS, constructors are just functions that happen to be called with the new operator in front of them. They are not attached to classes, nor are they instantiating a class. They are not even special types of functions. They're just regular functions that are, in essence, hijacked by the use of new in their invocation.

For example, consider the Number(..) function acting as a constructor, quoting from the ES5.1 spec:

15.7.2 The Number Constructor

When Number is called as part of a new expression it is a constructor: it initialises the newly created object.

So, pretty much any ol' function, including the built-in object functions like Number(..) (see Chapter 3) can be called with new in front of it, and that makes that function call a *constructor call*. This is an important but subtle distinction: there's really no such thing as "constructor functions," but rather construction calls *of* functions.

When a function is invoked with new in front of it, otherwise known as a constructor call, the following things are done automatically:

1. A brand new object is created (aka constructed) out of thin air.

2. The newly constructed object is [[Prototype]]-linked.

3. The newly constructed object is set as the this binding for that function call.

4. Unless the function returns its own alternate object, the new-invoked function call will *automatically* return the newly constructed object.

Steps 1, 3, and 4 apply to our current discussion. We'll skip over step 2 for now and come back to it in Chapter 5.

Consider this code:

```
function foo(a) {
    this.a = a;
}

var bar = new foo( 2 );
console.log( bar.a ); // 2
```

By calling foo(..) with new in front of it, we've constructed a new object and set that new object as the this for the call of foo(..). So new is the final way that a function call's this can be bound. We'll call this *new binding*.

Everything in Order

So, now we've uncovered the four rules for binding this in function calls. All you need to do is find the call-site and inspect it to see which rule applies. But, what if the call-site has multiple eligible rules? There must be an order of precedence to these rules, and so we will next demonstrate what order to apply the rules.

It should be clear that the *default binding* is the lowest priority rule of the four. So we'll just set that one aside.

Which is more precedent, *implicit binding* or *explicit binding*? Let's test it:

```
function foo() {
    console.log( this.a );
}

var obj1 = {
    a: 2,
    foo: foo
};

var obj2 = {
    a: 3,
    foo: foo
};
```

```
obj1.foo(); // 2
obj2.foo(); // 3

obj1.foo.call( obj2 ); // 3
obj2.foo.call( obj1 ); // 2
```

So, *explicit binding* takes precedence over *implicit binding*, which means you should ask first if *explicit binding* applies before checking for *implicit binding*.

Now, we just need to figure out where *new binding* fits in the precedence:

```
function foo(something) {
    this.a = something;
}

var obj1 = {
    foo: foo
};

var obj2 = {};

obj1.foo( 2 );
console.log( obj1.a ); // 2

obj1.foo.call( obj2, 3 );
console.log( obj2.a ); // 3

var bar = new obj1.foo( 4 );
console.log( obj1.a ); // 2
console.log( bar.a ); // 4
```

OK, *new binding* is more precedent than *implicit binding*. But do you think *new binding* is more or less precedent than *explicit binding*?

 new and call/apply cannot be used together, so new foo.call(obj1) is not allowed to test *new binding* directly against *explicit binding*. But we can still use a *hard binding* to test the precedence of the two rules.

Before we explore that in a code listing, think back to how *hard binding* physically works, which is that Function.prototype.bind(..) creates a new wrapper function that is hardcoded to ignore its own this binding (whatever it may be), and use a manual one we provide.

By that reasoning, it would seem obvious to assume that *hard binding* (which is a form of *explicit binding*) is more precedent than *new binding*, and thus cannot be overridden with new.

Let's check:

```
function foo(something) {
    this.a = something;
}

var obj1 = {};

var bar = foo.bind( obj1 );
bar( 2 );
console.log( obj1.a ); // 2

var baz = new bar( 3 );
console.log( obj1.a ); // 2
console.log( baz.a ); // 3
```

Whoa! bar is hard-bound against obj1, but new bar(3) did not change obj1.a to 3 as we would have expected. Instead, the hard-bound (to obj1) call to bar(..) *is* able to be overridden with new. Since new was applied, we got the newly created object back, which we named baz, and we see in fact that baz.a has the value 3.

This should be surprising if you go back to our "fake" bind helper:

```
function bind(fn, obj) {
    return function() {
        fn.apply( obj, arguments );
    };
}
```

If you think about how the helper's code works, it does not have a way for a new operator call to override the hard-binding to obj as we just observed.

But the built-in Function.prototype.bind(..) as of ES5 is more sophisticated, quite a bit so in fact. Here is the (slightly reformatted) polyfill provided by the MDN page for bind(..):

```
if (!Function.prototype.bind) {
    Function.prototype.bind = function(oThis) {
        if (typeof this !== "function") {
            // closest thing possible to the ECMAScript 5
            // internal IsCallable function
            throw new TypeError(
                "Function.prototype.bind - what is trying " +
                "to be bound is not callable"
```

```
                );
        }

        var aArgs = Array.prototype.slice.call( arguments, 1 ),
            fToBind = this,
            fNOP = function(){},
            fBound = function(){
                return fToBind.apply(
                    (
                        this instanceof fNOP &&
                        oThis ? this : oThis
                    ),
                    aArgs.concat(
                        Array.prototype.slice.call( arguments )
                    );
            }
        ;

        fNOP.prototype = this.prototype;
        fBound.prototype = new fNOP();

        return fBound;
    };
}
```

 The bind(..) polyfill shown above differs from the built-in bind(..) in ES5 with respect to hard-bound functions that will be used with new (read on to learn why that's useful). Because the polyfill cannot create a function without a .prototype as the built-in utility does, there's some nuanced indirection to approximate the same behavior. Tread carefully if you plan to use new with a hard-bound function and you rely on this polyfill.

The part that's allowing new overriding is:

```
this instanceof fNOP &&
oThis ? this : oThis

// ... and:

fNOP.prototype = this.prototype;
fBound.prototype = new fNOP();
```

We won't actually dive into explaining how this trickery works (it's complicated and beyond our scope here), but essentially the utility determines whether or not the hard-bound function has been called with new (resulting in a newly constructed object being its this), and if so, it uses *that* newly created `this` rather than the previously specified *hard binding* for `this`.

Why is `new` being able to override *hard binding* useful?

The primary reason for this behavior is to create a function (that can be used with `new` for constructing objects) that essentially ignores the `this` *hard binding*, but which presets some or all of the function's arguments. One of the capabilities of `bind(..)` is that any arguments passed after the first `this` binding argument are defaulted as standard arguments to the underlying function (technically called "partial application," which is a subset of "currying"). For example:

```
function foo(p1,p2) {
        this.val = p1 + p2;
}

// using `null` here because we don't care about
// the `this` hard-binding in this scenario, and
// it will be overridden by the `new` call anyway!
var bar = foo.bind( null, "p1" );

var baz = new bar( "p2" );

baz.val; // p1p2
```

Determining this

Now, we can summarize the rules for determining `this` from a function call's call-site, in their order of precedence. Ask these questions in this order, and stop when the first rule applies.

1. Is the function called with `new` (*new binding*)? If so, `this` is the newly constructed object.

    ```
    var bar = new foo()
    ```

2. Is the function called with `call` or `apply` (*explicit binding*), even hidden inside a `bind` *hard binding*? If so, `this` is the explicitly specified object.

    ```
    var bar = foo.call( obj2 )
    ```

3. Is the function called with a context (*implicit binding*), otherwise known as an owning or containing object? If so, `this` is *that* context object.

    ```
    var bar = obj1.foo()
    ```

4. Otherwise, default the this (*default binding*). If in strict mode, pick undefined, otherwise pick the global object.

```
var bar = foo()
```

That's it. That's *all it takes* to understand the rules of this binding for normal function calls. Well...almost.

Binding Exceptions

As usual, there are some exceptions to the "rules."

The this-binding behavior can in some scenarios be surprising, where you intended a different binding but you end up with binding behavior from the *default binding* rule.

Ignored this

If you pass null or undefined as a this binding parameter to call, apply, or bind, those values are effectively ignored, and instead the *default binding* rule applies to the invocation:

```
function foo() {
    console.log( this.a );
}

var a = 2;

foo.call( null ); // 2
```

Why would you intentionally pass something like null for a this binding?

It's quite common to use apply(..) for spreading out arrays of values as parameters to a function call. Similarly, bind(..) can curry parameters (preset values), which can be very helpful:

```
function foo(a,b) {
    console.log( "a:" + a + ", b:" + b );
}

// spreading out array as parameters
foo.apply( null, [2, 3] ); // a:2, b:3

// currying with `bind(..)`
var bar = foo.bind( null, 2 );
bar( 3 ); // a:2, b:3
```

Both these utilities require a `this` binding for the first parameter. If the functions in question don't care about `this`, you need a placeholder value, and `null` might seem like a reasonable choice as shown in this snippet.

 We don't cover it in this book, but ES6 has the `...` spread operator, which will let you syntactically "spread out" an array as parameters without needing `apply(..)`, such as `foo(...[1,2])`, which amounts to `foo(1,2)`—syntactically avoiding a `this` binding if it's unnecessary. Unfortunately, there's no ES6 syntactic substitute for currying, so the `this` parameter of the `bind(..)` call still needs attention.

However, there's a slight hidden "danger" in always using `null` when you don't care about the `this` binding. If you ever use that against a function call (for instance, a third-party library function that you don't control), and that function *does* make a `this` reference, the *default binding* rule means it might inadvertently reference (or worse, mutate!) the `global` object (`window` in the browser).

Obviously, such a pitfall can lead to a variety of bugs that are *very difficult* to diagnose and track down.

Safer this

Perhaps a somewhat "safer" practice is to pass a specifically set up object for `this` that is guaranteed not to be an object that can create problematic side effects in your program. Borrowing terminology from networking (and the military), we can create a "DMZ" (demilitarized zone) object—nothing more special than a completely empty, nondelegated object (see Chapters 5 and 6).

If we always pass a DMZ object for ignored `this` bindings we don't think we need to care about, we're sure any hidden/unexpected usage of `this` will be restricted to the empty object, which insulates our program's `global` object from side effects.

Since this object is totally empty, I personally like to give it the variable name ø (the lowercase mathematical symbol for the empty set). On many keyboards (like US-layout on Mac), this symbol is easily typed with ⌥+o (Option-o). Some systems also let you set up hotkeys for specific symbols. If you don't like the ø symbol, or your keyboard doesn't make it easy to type, you can of course call it whatever you want.

Whatever you call the variable, the easiest way to set it up as totally empty is `Object.create(null)` (see Chapter 5). `Object.create(null)` is similar to `{ }`, but without the delegation to `Object.prototype`, so it's "more empty" than just `{ }`:

```
function foo(a,b) {
    console.log( "a:" + a + ", b:" + b );
}

// our DMZ empty object
var ø = Object.create( null );

// spreading out array as parameters
foo.apply( ø, [2, 3] ); // a:2, b:3

// currying with `bind(..)`
var bar = foo.bind( ø, 2 );
bar( 3 ); // a:2, b:3
```

Not only is it functionally "safer," but there's a sort of stylistic benefit to ø, in that it semantically conveys "I want the `this` to be empty" a little more clearly than `null` might. But again, name your DMZ object whatever you prefer.

Indirection

Another thing to be aware of is that you can (intentionally or not!) create "indirect references" to functions, and in those cases, when that function reference is invoked, the *default binding* rule also applies.

One of the most common ways that *indirect references* occur is from an assignment:

```
function foo() {
    console.log( this.a );
}

var a = 2;
var o = { a: 3, foo: foo };
var p = { a: 4 };

o.foo(); // 3
(p.foo = o.foo)(); // 2
```

The *result value* of the assignment expression p.foo = o.foo is a reference to just the underlying function object. As such, the effective call-site is just foo( ), not p.foo( ) or o.foo( ) as you might expect. Per the rules mentioned earlier, the *default binding* rule applies.

Reminder: regardless of how you get to a function invocation using the *default binding* rule, the strict mode status of the contents of the invoked function making the this reference—not the function call-site—determines the *default binding* value: either the global object if in non-strict mode or undefined if in strict mode.

Softening Binding

We saw earlier that *hard binding* was one strategy for preventing a function call falling back to the *default binding* rule inadvertently, by forcing it to be bound to a specific this (unless you use new to override it!). The problem is, *hard binding* greatly reduces the flexibility of a function, preventing manual this override with either *implicit binding* or even subsequent *explicit binding* attempts.

It would be nice if there was a way to provide a different default for *default binding* (not global or undefined), while still leaving the function able to be manually this-bound via *implicit binding* or *explicit binding* techniques.

We can construct a so-called *soft binding* utility that emulates our desired behavior:

```
if (!Function.prototype.softBind) {
    Function.prototype.softBind = function(obj) {
        var fn = this;
        // capture any curried parameters
        var curried = [].slice.call( arguments, 1 );
        var bound = function() {
            return fn.apply(
                (!this || this === (window || global)) ?
                    obj : this
                curried.concat.apply( curried, arguments )
            );
        };
        bound.prototype = Object.create( fn.prototype );
        return bound;
    };
}
```

The softBind(..) utility provided here works similarly to the built-in ES5 bind(..) utility, except with our *soft binding* behavior. It wraps the specified function in logic that checks the this at call-time and if it's global or undefined, uses a prespecified alternate *default* (obj).

Otherwise the this is left untouched. It also provides optional currying (see the bind(..) discussion earlier).

Let's demonstrate its usage:

```
function foo() {
    console.log("name: " + this.name);
}

var obj = { name: "obj" },
    obj2 = { name: "obj2" },
    obj3 = { name: "obj3" };

var fooOBJ = foo.softBind( obj );

fooOBJ(); // name: obj

obj2.foo = foo.softBind(obj);
obj2.foo(); // name: obj2   <---- look!!!

fooOBJ.call( obj3 ); // name: obj3   <---- look!

setTimeout( obj2.foo, 10 );
// name: obj   <---- falls back to soft-binding
```

The soft-bound version of the foo() function can be manually this-bound to obj2 or obj3 as shown, but it falls back to obj if the *default binding* would otherwise apply.

Lexical this

Normal functions abide by the four rules we just covered. But ES6 introduces a special kind of function that does not use these rules: the arrow-function.

Arrow-functions are signified not by the function keyword, but by the so-called "fat arrow" operator, =>. Instead of using the four standard this rules, arrow-functions adopt the this binding from the enclosing (function or global) scope.

Let's illustrate the arrow-function lexical scope:

```
function foo() {
    // return an arrow function
    return (a) => {
        // `this` here is lexically inherited from `foo()`
        console.log( this.a );
    };
}
```

```
var obj1 = {
    a: 2
};

var obj2 = {
    a: 3
};

var bar = foo.call( obj1 );
bar.call( obj2 ); // 2, not 3!
```

The arrow-function created in foo() lexically captures whatever
foo()s this is at its call-time. Since foo() was this-bound to obj1,
bar (a reference to the returned arrow-function) will also be this-
bound to obj1. The lexical binding of an arrow-function cannot be
overridden (even with new!).

The most common use case will likely be in the use of callbacks, such
as event handlers or timers:

```
function foo() {
    setTimeout(() => {
        // `this` here is lexically inherited from `foo()`
        console.log( this.a );
    },100);
}

var obj = {
    a: 2
};

foo.call( obj ); // 2
```

While arrow-functions provide an alternative to using bind(..) on a
function to ensure its this, which can seem attractive, it's important
to note that they essentially are disabling the traditional this mechanism in favor of more widely understood lexical scoping. Pre-ES6, we
already have a fairly common pattern for doing so, which is basically
almost indistinguishable from the spirit of ES6 arrow-functions:

```
function foo() {
    var self = this; // lexical capture of `this`
    setTimeout( function(){
        console.log( self.a );
    }, 100 );
}

var obj = {
    a: 2
```

```
    };

    foo.call( obj ); // 2
```

While `self = this` and arrow-functions both seem like good "solutions" to not wanting to use `bind(..)`, they are essentially fleeing from `this` instead of understanding and embracing it.

If you find yourself writing `this`-style code, but most or all the time, you defeat the `this` mechanism with lexical `self = this` or arrow-function "tricks," perhaps you should either:

1. Use only lexical scope and forget the false pretense of `this`-style code.

2. Embrace `this`-style mechanisms completely, including using `bind(..)` where necessary, and try to avoid `self = this` and arrow-function "lexical this" tricks.

A program can effectively use both styles of code (lexical and `this`), but inside of the same function, and indeed for the same sorts of lookups, mixing the two mechanisms is usually asking for harder-to-maintain code, and probably working too hard to be clever.

Review

Determining the `this` binding for an executing function requires finding the direct call-site of that function. Once examined, four rules can be applied to the call-site, in *this* order of precedence:

1. Called with `new`? Use the newly constructed object.

2. Called with `call` or `apply` (or `bind`)? Use the specified object.

3. Called with a context object owning the call? Use that context object.

4. Default: `undefined` in `strict mode`, `global` object otherwise.

Be careful of accidental/unintentional invoking of the *default binding* rule. In cases where you want to "safely" ignore a `this` binding, a "DMZ" object like `ø = Object.create(null)` is a good placeholder value that protects the `global` object from unintended side effects.

Instead of the four standard binding rules, ES6 arrow-functions use lexical scoping for `this` binding, which means they inherit the `this` binding (whatever it is) from its enclosing function call. They are essentially a syntactic replacement of `self = this` in pre-ES6 coding.

CHAPTER 3

Objects

In Chapters 1 and 2, we explained how the `this` binding points to various objects depending on the call-site of the function invocation. But what exactly are objects, and why do we need to point to them? We will explore objects in detail in this chapter.

Syntax

Objects come in two forms: the declarative (literal) form and the constructed form.

The literal syntax for an object looks like this:

```
var myObj = {
    key: value
    // ...
};
```

The constructed form looks like this:

```
var myObj = new Object();
myObj.key = value;
```

The constructed form and the literal form result in exactly the same sort of object. The only difference really is that you can add one or more key/value pairs to the literal declaration, whereas with constructed-form objects, you must add the properties one by one.

It's extremely uncommon to use the "constructed form" for creating objects as just shown. You would pretty much always want to use the literal syntax form. The same will be true of most of the built-in objects (explained later).

Type

Objects are the general building block upon which much of JS is built. They are one of the six primary types (called "language types" in the specification) in JS:

- `string`
- `number`
- `boolean`
- `null`
- `undefined`
- `object`

Note that the *simple primitives* (`string`, `boolean`, `number`, `null`, and `undefined`) are not themselves `objects`. `null` is sometimes referred to as an object type, but this misconception stems from a bug in the language that causes `typeof null` to return the string `"object"` incorrectly (and confusingly). In fact, `null` is its own primitive type.

It's a common misstatement that "everything in JavaScript is an object." This is clearly not true.

By contrast, there *are* a few special object subtypes, which we can refer to as *complex primitives*.

`function` is a subtype of object (technically, a "callable object"). Functions in JS are said to be "first class" in that they are basically just normal objects (with callable behavior semantics bolted on), and so they can be handled like any other plain object.

Arrays are also a form of objects, with extra behavior. The organization of contents in arrays is slightly more structured than for general objects.

Built-in Objects

There are several other object subtypes, usually referred to as built-in objects. For some of them, their names seem to imply they are directly related to their simple primitive counterparts, but in fact, their relationship is more complicated, which we'll explore shortly.

- String
- Number
- Boolean
- Object
- Function
- Array
- Date
- RegExp
- Error

These built-ins have the appearance of being actual types, even classes, if you rely on the similarity to other languages such as Java's String class.

But in JS, these are actually just built-in functions. Each of these built-in functions can be used as a constructor (that is, a function call with the new operator—see Chapter 2), with the result being a newly *constructed* object of the subtype in question. For instance:

```
var strPrimitive = "I am a string";
typeof strPrimitive; // "string"
strPrimitive instanceof String; // false

var strObject = new String( "I am a string" );
typeof strObject; // "object"
strObject instanceof String; // true

// inspect the object sub-type
Object.prototype.toString.call( strObject ); // [object String]
```

We'll see in detail in a later chapter exactly how the Object.proto type.toString... bit works, but briefly, we can inspect the internal subtype by borrowing the base default toString() method, and you can see it reveals that strObject is an object that was in fact created by the String constructor.

The primitive value "I am a string" is not an object, it's a primitive literal and immutable value. To perform operations on it, such as checking its length, accessing its individual character contents, etc., a String object is required.

Luckily, the language automatically coerces a string primitive to a String object when necessary, which means you almost never need to explicitly create the Object form. It is strongly preferred by the majority of the JS community to use the literal form for a value, where possible, rather than the constructed object form.

Consider:

```
var strPrimitive = "I am a string";

console.log( strPrimitive.length ); // 13

console.log( strPrimitive.charAt( 3 ) ); // "m"
```

In both cases, we call a property or method on a string primitive, and the engine automatically coerces it to a String object, so that the property/method access works.

The same sort of coercion happens between the number literal primitive 42 and the new Number(42) object wrapper, when using methods like 42.359.toFixed(2). Likewise for Boolean objects from "boolean" primitives.

null and undefined have no object wrapper form, only their primitive values. By contrast, Date values can *only* be created with their constructed object form, as they have no literal form counterpart.

Objects, Arrays, Functions, and RegExps (regular expressions) are all objects regardless of whether the literal or constructed form is used. The constructed form does offer, in some cases, more options in creation than the literal form counterpart. Since objects are created either way, the simpler literal form is almost universally preferred. Only use the constructed form if you need the extra options.

Error objects are rarely created explicitly in code, but usually created automatically when exceptions are thrown. They can be created with the constructed form new Error(..), but it's often unnecessary.

Contents

As mentioned earlier, the contents of an object consist of values (any type) stored at specifically named *locations*, which we call properties.

It's important to note that while we say "contents," which implies that these values are *actually* stored inside the object, that's merely an appearance. The engine stores values in implementation-dependent ways, and may very well not store them *in* some object container. What *is* stored in the container are these property names, which act as pointers (technically, *references*) to where the values are stored.

Consider:

```
var myObject = {
    a: 2
};

myObject.a; // 2

myObject["a"]; // 2
```

To access the value at the *location* a in myObject, we need to use either the . operator or the [ ] operator. The .a syntax is usually referred to as "property access," whereas the ["a"] syntax is usually referred to as "key access." In reality, they both access the same *location* and will pull out the same value, 2, so the terms can be used interchangeably. We will use the most common term, "property access," from here on.

The main difference between the two syntaxes is that the . operator requires an Identifier-compatible property name after it, whereas the [".."] syntax can take basically any UTF-8/Unicode-compatible string as the name for the property. To reference a property of the name "Super-Fun!", for instance, you would have to use the ["Super-Fun!"] access syntax, as Super-Fun! is not a valid Identifier property name.

Also, since the [".."] syntax uses a string's value to specify the location, this means the program can programmatically build up the value of the string, such as:

```
var myObject = {
    a: 2
};

var idx;
```

```
if (wantA) {
    idx = "a";
}

// later

console.log( myObject[idx] ); // 2
```

In objects, property names are *always* strings. If you use any other
value besides a string (primitive) as the property, it will first be con-
verted to a string. This even includes numbers, which are commonly
used as array indexes, so be careful not to confuse the use of numbers
between objects and arrays:

```
var myObject = { };

myObject[true] = "foo";
myObject[3] = "bar";
myObject[myObject] = "baz";

myObject["true"]; // "foo"
myObject["3"]; // "bar"
myObject["[object Object]"]; // "baz"
```

Computed Property Names

The myObject[..] property access syntax we just described is useful
if you need to use a computed expression value *as* the key name, like
myObject[prefix + name]. But that's not really helpful when declaring objects using the object-literal syntax.

ES6 adds *computed property names*, where you can specify an expression, surrounded by a [ ] pair, in the key-name position of an object-
literal declaration:

```
var prefix = "foo";

var myObject = {
    [prefix + "bar"]: "hello",
    [prefix + "baz"]: "world"
};

myObject["foobar"]; // hello
myObject["foobaz"]; // world
```

The most common usage of *computed property names* will probably
be for ES6 Symbols, which we will not be covering in detail in this book.
In short, they're a new primitive data type that has an opaque un-
guessable value (technically a string value). You will be strongly

discouraged from working with the *actual value* of a `Symbol` (which can theoretically be different between different JS engines), so the name of the `Symbol`, like `Symbol.Something` (just a made up name!), will be what you use:

```
var myObject = {
    [Symbol.Something]: "hello world"
};
```

Property Versus Method

Some developers like to make a distinction when talking about a property access on an object, if the value being accessed happens to be a function. Because it's tempting to think of the function as *belonging* to the object, and in other languages, functions that belong to objects (aka "classes") are referred to as "methods," it's not uncommon to hear "method access" as opposed to "property access."

The specification makes this same distinction, interestingly.

Technically, functions never "belong" to objects, so saying that a function that just happens to be accessed on an object reference is automatically a "method" seems a bit of a stretch of semantics.

It *is* true that some functions have `this` references in them, and that *sometimes* these `this` references refer to the object reference at the call-site. But this usage really does not make that function any more a "method" than any other function, as `this` is dynamically bound at runtime, at the call-site, and thus its relationship to the object is indirect, at best.

Every time you access a property on an object, that is a property access, regardless of the type of value you get back. If you happen to get a function from that property access, it's not magically a "method" at that point. There's nothing special (outside of possible implicit `this` binding as explained earlier) about a function that comes from a property access.

For instance:

```
function foo() {
    console.log( "foo" );
}

var someFoo = foo; // variable reference to `foo`

var myObject = {
```

```
    someFoo: foo
};

foo; // function foo(){..}

someFoo; // function foo(){..}

myObject.someFoo; // function foo(){..}
```

someFoo and myObject.someFoo are just two separate references to the same function, and neither implies anything about the function being special or "owned" by any other object. If foo() was defined to have a this reference inside it, that myObject.someFoo *implicit binding* would be the only observable difference between the two references. It doesn't make sense to call either reference a "method."

Perhaps one could argue that a function becomes a method, not at definition time, but during runtime just for that invocation, depending on how it's called at its call-site (with or without an object reference context—see Chapter 2 for more details). Even this interpretation is a bit of a stretch.

The safest conclusion is probably that "function" and "method" are interchangeable in JavaScript.

 ES6 adds a super reference, which is typically going to be used with class (see Appendix A). The way super behaves (static binding rather than late binding as this) gives further weight to the idea that a function that is super-bound somewhere is more a "method" than "function." But again, these are just subtle semantic (and mechanical) nuances.

Even when you declare a function expression as part of the object literal, that function doesn't magically *belong* more to the object— there are still just multiple references to the same function object:

```
var myObject = {
    foo: function() {
        console.log( "foo" );
    }
};

var someFoo = myObject.foo;

someFoo; // function foo(){..}

myObject.foo; // function foo(){..}
```

In Chapter 6, we will cover an ES6 shorthand for that `foo:`
`function(){ .. }` declaration syntax in our object literal.

Arrays

Arrays also use the [ ] access form, but as mentioned earlier, they have
slightly more structured organization for how and where values are
stored (though still no restriction on what *type* of values are stored).
Arrays assume *numeric indexing*, which means that values are stored
in locations, usually called *indices*, at positive integers, such as 0 and 42:

```
var myArray = [ "foo", 42, "bar" ];

myArray.length; // 3

myArray[0]; // "foo"

myArray[2]; // "bar"
```

Arrays *are* objects, so even though each index is a positive integer, you
can *also* add properties onto the array:

```
var myArray = [ "foo", 42, "bar" ];

myArray.baz = "baz";

myArray.length; // 3

myArray.baz; // "baz"
```

Notice that adding named properties (regardless of . or [ ] operator
syntax) does not change the reported `length` of the array.

You *could* use an array as a plain key/value object, and never add any
numeric indices, but this is bad idea because arrays have behavior and
optimizations specific to their intended use, and likewise with plain
objects. Use objects to store key/value pairs, and arrays to store values
at numeric indices.

Be careful: if you try to add a property to an array, but the property
name *looks* like a number, it will end up instead as a numeric index
(thus modifying the array contents):

```
var myArray = [ "foo", 42, "bar" ];

myArray["3"] = "baz";

myArray.length; // 4

myArray[3]; // "baz"
```

Duplicating Objects

One of the most commonly requested features when developers newly take up the JavaScript language is how to duplicate an object. It would seem like there should just be a built-in copy() method, right? It turns out that it's a little more complicated than that, because it's not fully clear what, by default, should be the algorithm for the duplication.

For example, consider this object:

```
function anotherFunction() { /*..*/ }

var anotherObject = {
    c: true
};

var anotherArray = [];

var myObject = {
    a: 2,
    b: anotherObject, // reference, not a copy!
    c: anotherArray, // another reference!
    d: anotherFunction
};

anotherArray.push( anotherObject, myObject );
```

What exactly should be the representation of a *copy* of myObject?

First, we should answer if it should be a *shallow* or *deep* copy? A *shallow copy* would end up with a on the new object as a copy of the value 2, but the b, c, and d properties as just references to the same places as the references in the original object. A *deep copy* would duplicate not only myObject, but anotherObject and anotherArray. But then we have the issue that anotherArray has references to anotherObject and myObject in it, so *those* should also be duplicated rather than reference-preserved. Now we have an infinite circular duplication problem because of the circular reference.

Should we detect a circular reference and just break the circular traversal (leaving the deep element not fully duplicated)? Should we error out completely? Something in between?

Moreover, it's not really clear what "duplicating" a function would mean. There are some hacks like pulling out the `toString()` serialization of a function's source code (which varies across implementations and is not even reliable in all engines depending on the type of function being inspected).

So how do we resolve all these tricky questions? Various JS frameworks have each picked their own interpretations and made their own decisions. But which of these (if any) should JS adopt as *the* standard? For a long time, there was no clear answer.

One subset solution is that objects that are JSON-safe (that is, can be serialized to a JSON string and then reparsed to an object with the same structure and values) can easily be *duplicated* with:

```
var newObj = JSON.parse( JSON.stringify( someObj ) );
```

Of course, that requires you to ensure your object is JSON-safe. For some situations, that's trivial. For others, it's insufficient.

At the same time, a shallow copy is fairly understandable and has far fewer issues, so ES6 has now defined `Object.assign(..)` for this task. `Object.assign(..)` takes a *target* object as its first parameter, and one or more *source* objects as its subsequent parameters. It iterates over all the *enumerable* (see the following code), *owned keys* (immediately present) on the *source* object(s) and copies them (via = assignment only) to the *target*. It also, helpfully, returns the *target*, as you can see here:

```
var newObj = Object.assign( {}, myObject );

newObj.a; // 2
newObj.b === anotherObject; // true
newObj.c === anotherArray; // true
newObj.d === anotherFunction; // true
```

 In the next section, we describe "property descriptors" (property characteristics) and show the use of `Object.defineProp erty(..)`. The duplication that occurs for `Object.as sign(..)`, however, is purely = style assignment, so any special characteristics of a property (like `writable`) on a source object are not preserved on the target object.

Property Descriptors

Prior to ES5, the JavaScript language gave no direct way for your code to inspect or draw any distinction between the characteristics of properties, such as whether the property was read-only or not.

But as of ES5, all properties are described in terms of a *property descriptor*.

Consider this code:

```
var myObject = {
    a: 2
};

Object.getOwnPropertyDescriptor( myObject, "a" );
// {
//     value: 2,
//     writable: true,
//     enumerable: true,
//     configurable: true
// }
```

As you can see, the property descriptor (called a "data descriptor" since it's only for holding a data value) for our normal object property a is much more than just its value of 2. It includes three other characteristics: writable, enumerable, and configurable.

While we can see what the default values for the property descriptor characteristics are when we create a normal property, we can use Object.defineProperty(..) to add a new property, or modify an existing one (if it's configurable!), with the desired characteristics.

For example:

```
var myObject = {};

Object.defineProperty( myObject, "a", {
    value: 2,
    writable: true,
    configurable: true,
    enumerable: true
} );

myObject.a; // 2
```

Using defineProperty(..), we added the plain, normal a property to myObject in a manually explicit way. However, you generally wouldn't use this manual approach unless you wanted to modify one of the descriptor characteristics from its normal behavior.

Writable

The ability for you to change the value of a property is controlled by `writable`.

Consider:

```
var myObject = {};

Object.defineProperty( myObject, "a", {
    value: 2,
    writable: false, // not writable!
    configurable: true,
    enumerable: true
} );

myObject.a = 3;

myObject.a; // 2
```

As you can see, our modification of the `value` silently failed. If we try in `strict` mode, we get an error:

```
"use strict";

var myObject = {};

Object.defineProperty( myObject, "a", {
    value: 2,
    writable: false, // not writable!
    configurable: true,
    enumerable: true
} );

myObject.a = 3; // TypeError
```

The `TypeError` tells us we cannot change a nonwritable property.

 We will discuss getters/setters shortly, but briefly, you can observe that `writable:false` means a value cannot be changed, which is somewhat equivalent to if you defined a no-op setter. Actually, your no-op setter would need to throw a `TypeError` when called to be truly conformant to `writable:false`.

Configurable

As long as a property is currently configurable, we can modify its descriptor definition, using the same `defineProperty(..)` utility:

```
var myObject = {
    a: 2
};

myObject.a = 3;
myObject.a;    // 3

Object.defineProperty( myObject, "a", {
    value: 4,
    writable: true,
    configurable: false,    // not configurable!
    enumerable: true
} );

myObject.a;    // 4
myObject.a = 5;
myObject.a;    // 5

Object.defineProperty( myObject, "a", {
    value: 6,
    writable: true,
    configurable: true,
    enumerable: true
} );    // TypeError
```

The final `defineProperty(..)` call results in a `TypeError`, regardless of `strict` mode, if you attempt to change the descriptor definition of a nonconfigurable property. Be careful: as you can see, changing configurable to `false` is a one-way action, and cannot be undone!

There's a nuanced exception to be aware of: even if the property is already `configurable:false`, `writable` can always be changed from `true` to `false` without error, but not back to `true` if already `false`.

Another thing `configurable:false` prevents is the ability to use the `delete` operator to remove an existing property:

```
var myObject = {
    a: 2
};

myObject.a;    // 2
```

```
delete myObject.a;
myObject.a; // undefined

Object.defineProperty( myObject, "a", {
    value: 2,
    writable: true,
    configurable: false,
    enumerable: true
} );

myObject.a; // 2
delete myObject.a;
myObject.a; // 2
```

As you can see, the last `delete` call failed (silently) because we made the a property nonconfigurable.

`delete` is only used to remove object properties (which can be removed) directly from the object in question. If an object property is the last remaining *reference* to some object/function, and you `delete` it, that removes the reference and now that unreferenced object/ function can be garbage-collected. But, it is not proper to think of `delete` as a tool to free up allocated memory as it does in other languages (like C/C++). `delete` is just an object property removal operation—nothing more.

Enumerable

The final descriptor characteristic we will mention here (there are two others, which we deal with shortly when we discuss getter/setters) is `enumerable`.

The name probably makes it obvious, but this characteristic controls whether a property will show up in certain object-property enumerations, such as the `for..in` loop. Set `enumerable` to `false` to keep the property from showing up in such enumerations, even though it's still completely accessible. Set it to `true` to include the property in enumerations.

All normal user-defined properties are defaulted to `enumerable`, as this is most commonly what you want. But if you have a special property you want to hide from enumeration, set it to `enumerable:false`.

We'll demonstrate enumerability in much more detail shortly, so keep a mental bookmark on this topic.

Immutability

Sometimes you want to make properties or objects that cannot be changed (either by accident or intentionally). ES5 adds support for handling that in a variety of different nuanced ways.

It's important to note that *all* of these approaches create shallow immutability. That is, they affect only the object and its direct property characteristics. If an object has a reference to another object (array, object, function, etc.), the *contents* of that object are not affected and remain mutable:

```
myImmutableObject.foo; // [1,2,3]
myImmutableObject.foo.push( 4 );
myImmutableObject.foo; // [1,2,3,4]
```

We assume in this snippet that `myImmutableObject` is already created and protected as immutable. But, to also protect the contents of `myImmutableObject.foo` (which is its own object—an array), you would also need to make `foo` immutable, using one or more of the following functionalities.

 It is not terribly common to create deeply entrenched immutable objects in JS programs. Special cases can certainly call for it, but as a general design pattern, if you find yourself wanting to *seal* or *freeze* all your objects, you may want to take a step back and reconsider your program design to be more robust to potential changes in objects' values.

Object constant

By combining `writable:false` and `configurable:false`, you can essentially create a *constant* (cannot be changed, redefined, or deleted) as an object property, like:

```
var myObject = {};

Object.defineProperty( myObject, "FAVORITE_NUMBER", {
    value: 42,
    writable: false,
    configurable: false
} );
```

Prevent extensions

If you want to prevent an object from having new properties added to it, but otherwise leave the rest of the object's properties alone, call `Object.preventExtensions(..)`:

```
var myObject = {
    a: 2
};

Object.preventExtensions( myObject );

myObject.b = 3;
myObject.b; // undefined
```

In non-`strict` mode, the creation of b fails silently. In `strict` mode, it throws a `TypeError`.

Seal

`Object.seal(..)` creates a "sealed" object, which means it takes an existing object and essentially calls `Object.preventExtensions(..)` on it, but also marks all its existing properties as `configurable:false`.

So, not only can you not add any more properties, but you also cannot reconfigure or delete any existing properties (though you *can* still modify their values).

Freeze

`Object.freeze(..)` creates a frozen object, which means it takes an existing object and essentially calls `Object.seal(..)` on it, but it also marks all "data accessor" properties as `writable:false`, so that their values cannot be changed.

This approach is the highest level of immutability that you can attain for an object itself, as it prevents any changes to the object or to any of its direct properties (though, as mentioned earlier, the contents of any referenced other objects are unaffected).

You could "deep freeze" an object by calling `Object.freeze(..)` on the object, and then recursively iterating over all objects it references (which would have been unaffected thus far), and calling `Object.freeze(..)` on them as well. Be careful, though, as that could affect other (shared) objects you're not intending to affect.

[[Get]]

There's a subtle, but important, detail about how property accesses are performed. Consider:

```
var myObject = {
    a: 2
};

myObject.a; // 2
```

The myObject.a is a property access, but it doesn't *just* look in myObject for a property of the name a, as it might seem.

According to the spec, the previous code actually performs a [[Get]] operation (kinda like a function call: [[Get]]()) on the myObject. The default built-in [[Get]] operation for an object *first* inspects the object for a property of the requested name, and if it finds it, it will return the value accordingly.

However, the [[Get]] algorithm defines other important behavior if it does *not* find a property of the requested name. We will examine in Chapter 5 what happens *next* (traversal of the [[Prototype]] chain, if any).

But one important result of this [[Get]] operation is that if it cannot through any means come up with a value for the requested property, it instead returns the value undefined:

```
var myObject = {
    a: 2
};

myObject.b; // undefined
```

This behavior is different from when you reference *variables* by their identifier names. If you reference a variable that cannot be resolved within the applicable lexical scope lookup, the result is not undefined as it is for object properties, but instead a ReferenceError is thrown:

```
var myObject = {
    a: undefined
};

myObject.a; // undefined

myObject.b; // undefined
```

From a *value* perspective, there is no difference between these two references—they both result in undefined. However, the [[Get]] operation underneath, though subtle at a glance, potentially performed a bit more "work" for the reference myObject.b than for the reference myObject.a.

Inspecting only the value results, you cannot distinguish whether a property exists and holds the explicit value undefined, or whether the property does *not* exist and undefined was the default return value after [[Get]] failed to return something explicitly. However, we will see shortly how you *can* distinguish these two scenarios.

[[Put]]

Since there's an internally defined [[Get]] operation for getting a value from a property, it should be obvious there's also a default [[Put]] operation.

It may be tempting to think that an assignment to a property on an object would just invoke [[Put]] to set or create that property on the object in question. But the situation is more nuanced than that.

When invoking [[Put]], how it behaves differs based on a number of factors, including (most impactfully) whether the property is already present on the object or not.

If the property is present, the [[Put]] algorithm will roughly check:

1. Is the property an accessor descriptor (see "Getters and Setters" on page 54)? If so, call the setter, if any.

2. Is the property a data descriptor with writable of false? If so, silently fail in non-strict mode, or throw TypeError in strict mode.

3. Otherwise, set the value to the existing property as normal.

If the property is not yet present on the object in question, the [[Put]] operation is even more nuanced and complex. We will revisit this scenario in Chapter 5 when we discuss [[Prototype]] to give it more clarity.

Getters and Setters

The default [[Put]] and [[Get]] operations for objects completely control how values are set to existing or new properties, or retrieved from existing properties, respectively.

 Using future/advanced capabilities of the language, it may be possible to override the default [[Get]] or [[Put]] operations for an entire object (not just per property). This is beyond the scope of our discussion in this book, but may be covered later in the *You Don't Know JS* series.

ES5 introduced a way to override part of these default operations, not on an object level but a per-property level, through the use of getters and setters. Getters are properties that actually call a hidden function to retrieve a value. Setters are properties that actually call a hidden function to set a value.

When you define a property to have either a getter or a setter or both, its definition becomes an "accessor descriptor" (as opposed to a "data descriptor"). For accessor desciptors, the value and writable characteristics of the descriptor are moot and ignored, and instead JS considers the set and get characteristics of the property (as well as con figurable and enumerable).

Consider:

```
var myObject = {
    // define a getter for `a`
    get a() {
        return 2;
    }
};

Object.defineProperty(
    myObject,    // target
    "b",         // property name
    {            // descriptor
        // define a getter for `b`
        get: function(){ return this.a * 2 },

        // make sure `b` shows up as an object property
        enumerable: true
    }
);

myObject.a; // 2
```

```
myObject.b; // 4
```

Either through object-literal syntax with `get a() { .. }` or through explicit definition with `defineProperty(..)`, in both cases we created a property on the object that actually doesn't hold a value, but whose access automatically results in a hidden function call to the getter function, with whatever value it returns being the result of the property access:

```
var myObject = {
    // define a getter for `a`
    get a() {
        return 2;
    }
};

myObject.a = 3;

myObject.a; // 2
```

Since we only defined a getter for a, if we try to set the value of a later, the `set` operation won't throw an error but will just silently throw the assignment away. Even if there was a valid setter, our custom getter is hardcoded to return only 2, so the `set` operation would be moot.

To make this scenario more sensible, properties should also be defined with setters, which override the default `[[Put]]` operation (aka assignment), per-property, just as you'd expect. You will almost certainly want to always declare both getter and setter (having only one or the other often leads to unexpected/surprising behavior):

```
var myObject = {
    // define a getter for `a`
    get a() {
        return this._a_;
    },

    // define a setter for `a`
    set a(val) {
        this._a_ = val * 2;
    }
};

myObject.a = 2;

myObject.a; // 4
```

In this example, we actually store the specified value 2 of the assigment ([[Put]] operation) into another variable _a_. The _a_ name is purely by convention for this example and implies nothing special about its behavior—it's a normal property like any other.

Existence

We showed earlier that a property access like myObject.a may result in an undefined value if either the explicit undefined is stored there or the a property doesn't exist at all. So, if the value is the same in both cases, how else do we distinguish them?

We can ask an object if it has a certain property *without* asking to get that property's value:

```
var myObject = {
    a: 2
};

("a" in myObject); // true
("b" in myObject); // false

myObject.hasOwnProperty( "a" ); // true
myObject.hasOwnProperty( "b" ); // false
```

The in operator will check to see if the property is *in* the object, or if it exists at any higher level of the [[Prototype]] chain object traversal (see Chapter 5). By contrast, hasOwnProperty(..) checks to see if *only* myObject has the property or not, and will *not* consult the [[Prototype]] chain. We'll come back to the important differences between these two operations in Chapter 5 when we explore [[Prototype]]s in detail.

hasOwnProperty(..) is accessible for all normal objects via delegation to Object.prototype (see Chapter 5). But it's possible to create an object that does not link to Object.prototype (via Object.create(null)—see Chapter 5). In this case, a method call like myObject.hasOwnProperty(..) would fail.

In that scenario, a more robust way of performing such a check is Object.prototype.hasOwnProperty.call(myObject,"a"), which borrows the base hasOwnProperty(..) method and uses *explicit binding* (see Chapter 2) to apply it against our myObject.

It appears that the in operator will check for the existence of a *value* inside a container, but it actually checks for the existence of a property name. This difference is important to note with respect to arrays, as the temptation to try a check like 4 in [2, 4, 6] is strong, but this will not behave as expected.

Enumeration

Previously, we explained briefly the idea of "enumerability" when we looked at the enumerable property descriptor characteristic. Let's revisit that and examine it in closer detail:

```
var myObject = { };

Object.defineProperty(
    myObject,
    "a",
    // make `a` enumerable, as normal
    { enumerable: true, value: 2 }
);

Object.defineProperty(
    myObject,
    "b",
    // make `b` NON-enumerable
    { enumerable: false, value: 3 }
);

myObject.b; // 3
("b" in myObject); // true
myObject.hasOwnProperty( "b" ); // true

// .......

for (var k in myObject) {
    console.log( k, myObject[k] );
}
// "a" 2
```

You'll notice that myObject.b in fact exists and has an accessible value, but it doesn't show up in a for..in loop (though, surprisingly, it is revealed by the in operator existence check). That's because "enumerable" basically means "will be included if the object's properties are iterated through."

for..in loops applied to arrays can give somewhat unexpected results, in that the enumeration of an array will include not only all the numeric indices, but also any enumerable properties. It's a good idea to use for..in loops *only* on objects, and traditional for loops with numeric index iteration for arrays.

Consider another way that enumerable and nonenumerable properties can be distinguished:

```
var myObject = { };

Object.defineProperty(
    myObject,
    "a",
    // make `a` enumerable, as normal
    { enumerable: true, value: 2 }
);

Object.defineProperty(
    myObject,
    "b",
    // make `b` nonenumerable
    { enumerable: false, value: 3 }
);

myObject.propertyIsEnumerable( "a" ); // true
myObject.propertyIsEnumerable( "b" ); // false

Object.keys( myObject ); // ["a"]
Object.getOwnPropertyNames( myObject ); // ["a", "b"]
```

propertyIsEnumerable(..) tests whether the given property name exists *directly* on the object and is also enumerable:true.

Object.keys(..) returns an array of all enumerable properties, whereas Object.getOwnPropertyNames(..) returns an array of *all* properties, enumerable or not.

Whereas in versus hasOwnProperty(..) differ in whether they consult the [[Prototype]] chain or not, Object.keys(..) and Object.getOwnPropertyNames(..) both inspect *only* the direct object specified.

There's (currently) no built-in way to get a list of all properties that is equivalent to what the in operator test would consult (traversing all properties on the entire [[Prototype]] chain, as explained in Chapter 5). You could approximate such a utility by recursively traversing the [[Prototype]] chain of an object, and for each level, capturing the list from Object.keys(..)—only enumerable properties.

Iteration

The for..in loop iterates over the list of enumerable properties on an object (including its [[Prototype]] chain). But what if you instead want to iterate over the values?

With numerically indexed arrays, iterating over the values is typically done with a standard for loop, like:

```
var myArray = [1, 2, 3];

for (var i = 0; i < myArray.length; i++) {
    console.log( myArray[i] );
}
// 1 2 3
```

This isn't iterating over the values, though, but iterating over the indices, where you then use the index to reference the value, as myArray[i].

ES5 also added several iteration helpers for arrays, including forEach(..), every(..), and some(..). Each of these helpers accepts a function callback to apply to each element in the array, differing only in how they respectively respond to a return value from the callback.

forEach(..) will iterate over all values in the array, and it ignores any callback return values. every(..) keeps going until the end *or* the callback returns a false (or "falsy") value, whereas some(..) keeps going until the end *or* the callback returns a true (or "truthy") value.

These special return values inside every(..) and some(..) act somewhat like a **break** statement inside a normal for loop, in that they stop the iteration early before it reaches the end.

If you iterate on an object with a for..in loop, you're also only getting at the values indirectly, because it's actually iterating only over the enumerable properties of the object, leaving you to access the properties manually to get the values.

As contrasted with iterating over an array's indices in a numerically ordered way (`for` loop or other iterators), the order of iteration over an object's properties is not guaranteed and may vary between different JS engines. Do not rely on any observed ordering for anything that requires consistency among environments, as any observed agreement is unreliable.

But what if you want to iterate over the values directly instead of the array indicies (or object properties)? Helpfully, ES6 adds a `for..of` loop syntax for iterating over arrays (and objects, if the object defines its own custom iterator):

```
var myArray = [ 1, 2, 3 ];

for (var v of myArray) {
    console.log( v );
}
// 1
// 2
// 3
```

The `for..of` loop asks for an iterator object (from a default internal function known as `@@iterator` in spec-speak) of the *thing* to be iterated, and the loop then iterates over the successive return values from calling that iterator object's `next()` method, once for each loop iteration.

Arrays have a built-in `@@iterator`, so `for..of` works easily on them, as shown. But let's manually iterate the array, using the built-in `@@iterator`, to see how it works:

```
var myArray = [ 1, 2, 3 ];
var it = myArray[Symbol.iterator]();

it.next(); // { value:1, done:false }
it.next(); // { value:2, done:false }
it.next(); // { value:3, done:false }
it.next(); // { done:true }
```

We get at the `@@iterator` *internal property* of an object using an ES6 Symbol: `Symbol.iterator`. We briefly mentioned Symbol semantics earlier in the chapter (see "Computed Property Names" on page 40), so the same reasoning applies here. You'll always want to reference such special properties by `Symbol` name reference instead of by the special value it may hold. Also, despite the name's implications, `@@iterator` is not the iterator object itself, but a function that returns the iterator object —a subtle but important detail!

As the previous snippet reveals, the return value from an iterator's `next()` call is an object of the form `{ value: .. , done: .. }`, where `value` is the current iteration value, and `done` is a `boolean` that indicates whether there's more to iterate.

Notice the value 3 was returned with a `done:false`, which seems strange at first glance. You have to call the `next()` a fourth time (which the `for..of` loop in the previous snippet automatically does) to get `done:true` and know you're truly done iterating. The reason for this quirk is beyond the scope of what we'll discuss here, but it comes from the semantics of ES6 generator functions.

While arrays do automatically iterate in `for..of` loops, regular objects do not have a built-in `@@iterator`. The reasons for this intentional omission are more complex than we will examine here, but in general, it was better to not include some implementation that could prove troublesome for future types of objects.

It *is* possible to define your own default `@@iterator` for any object that you care to iterate over. For example:

```
var myObject = {
    a: 2,
    b: 3
};

Object.defineProperty( myObject, Symbol.iterator, {
    enumerable: false,
    writable: false,
    configurable: true,
    value: function() {
        var o = this;
        var idx = 0;
        var ks = Object.keys( o );
        return {
            next: function() {
```

```
            return {
                value: o[ks[idx++]],
                done: (idx > ks.length)
            };
        }
    };
    }
} );

// iterate `myObject` manually
var it = myObject[Symbol.iterator]();
it.next(); // { value:2, done:false }
it.next(); // { value:3, done:false }
it.next(); // { value:undefined, done:true }

// iterate `myObject` with `for..of`
for (var v of myObject) {
    console.log( v );
}
// 2
// 3
```

We used Object.defineProperty(..) to define our custom
@@iterator (mostly so we could make it nonenumerable), but
using the Symbol as a *computed property name* (covered earlier in this chapter), we could have declared it directly, like var
myObject = { a:2, b:3, [Symbol.iterator]: function()
{ /* .. */ } }.

Each time the for..of loop calls next() on myObject's iterator object,
the internal pointer will advance and return back the next value from
the object's properties list (see the note earlier in this section about
iteration ordering on object properties/values).

The iteration we just demonstrated is a simple value-by-value iteration, but you can of course define arbitrarily complex iterations for
your custom data structures, as you see fit. Custom iterators combined
with ES6's for..of loop are a powerful new syntactic tool for manip-
ulating user-defined objects.

For example, a list of Pixel objects (with x and y coordinate values)
could decide to order its iteration based on the linear distance from
the (0,0) origin, or filter out points that are "too far away," etc. As long
as your iterator returns the expected { value: .. } return values
from next() calls, and a { done: true } after the iteration is complete, ES6's for..of can iterate over it.

In fact, you can even define "infinite" iterators that never "finish" and always return a new value (such as a random number, an incremented value, a unique identifier, etc.), though you probably will not use such iterators with an unbounded `for..of` loop, as it would never end and would hang your program:

```
var randoms = {
    [Symbol.iterator]: function() {
        return {
            next: function() {
                return { value: Math.random() };
            }
        };
    }
};

var randoms_pool = [];
for (var n of randoms) {
    randoms_pool.push( n );

    // don't proceed unbounded!
    if (randoms_pool.length === 100) break;
}
```

This iterator will generate random numbers "forever," so we're careful to only pull out 100 values so our program doesn't hang.

Review

Objects in JS have both a literal form (such as `var a = { .. }`) and a constructed form (such as `var a = new Array(..)`). The literal form is almost always preferred, but the constructed form offers, in some cases, more creation options.

Many people mistakenly claim "everything in JavaScript is an object," but this is incorrect. Objects are one of the six (or seven, depending on your perspective) primitive types. Objects have subtypes, including `function`, and also can be behavior-specialized, like `[object Array]` as the internal label representing the array object subtype.

Objects are collections of key/value pairs. The values can be accessed as properties, via the `.propName` or `["propName"]` syntax. Whenever a property is accessed, the engine actually invokes the internal default `[[Get]]` operation (and `[[Put]]` for setting values), which not only looks for the property directly on the object, but will traverse the `[[Prototype]]` chain (see Chapter 5) if not found.

Properties have certain characteristics that can be controlled through property descriptors, such as `writable` and `configurable`. In addition, objects can have their mutability (and that of their properties) controlled to various levels of immutability using `Object.preventEx tensions(..)`, `Object.seal(..)`, and `Object.freeze(..)`.

Properties don't have to contain values—they can be "accessor properties" as well, with getters/setters. They can also be either *enumerable* or not, which controls whether they show up in `for..in` loop iterations, for instance.

You can also iterate over the values in data structures (arrays, objects, etc.) using the ES6 `for..of` syntax, which looks for either a built-in or custom `@@iterator` object consisting of a `next()` method to advance through the data values one at a time.

CHAPTER 4

Mixing (Up) "Class" Objects

Following our exploration of objects from the previous chapter, it's natural that we now turn our attention to object-oriented (OO) programming, with classes. We'll first look at class orientation as a design pattern, before examining the mechanics of classes: instantiation, inheritance, and (relative) polymorphism.

We'll see that these concepts don't really map very naturally to the object mechanism in JS, and the efforts (mixins, etc.) many JavaScript developers expend to overcome such challenges.

 This chapter spends quite a bit of time (the first half!) on heavy object-oriented programming theory. We eventually relate these ideas to real concrete JavaScript code in the second half, when we talk about mixins. But there's a lot of concept and pseudocode to wade through first, so don't get lost—just stick with it!

Class Theory

Class/inheritance describes a certain form of code organization and architecture—a way of modeling real world problem domains in our software.

OO or class-oriented programming stresses that data intrinsically has associated behavior (of course, different depending on the type and nature of the data!) that operates on it, so proper design is to package up (aka encapsulate) the data and the behavior together. This is sometimes called *data structures* in formal computer science.

For example, a series of characters that represents a word or phrase is usually called a *string*. The characters are the data. But you almost never just care about the data, you usually want to *do things* with the data, so the behaviors that can apply *to* that data (calculating its length, appending data, searching, etc.) are all designed as methods of a `String` class.

Any given string is just an instance of this class, which means that it's a neatly collected packaging of both the character data and the functionality we can perform on it.

Classes also imply a way of *classifying* a certain data structure. The way we do this is to think about any given structure as a specific variation of a more general base definition.

Let's explore this classification process by looking at a commonly cited example. A *car* can be described as a specific implementation of a more general "class" of thing, called a *vehicle*.

We model this relationship in software with classes by defining a `Vehicle` class and a `Car` class.

The definition of `Vehicle` might include things like propulsion (engines, etc.), the ability to carry people, etc., which would all be the behaviors. What we define in `Vehicle` is all the stuff that is common to all (or most of) the different types of vehicles (the "planes, trains, and automobiles").

It might not make sense in our software to redefine the basic essence of "ability to carry people" over and over again for each different type of vehicle. Instead, we define that capability once in `Vehicle`, and then when we define `Car`, we simply indicate that it *inherits* (or *extends*) the base definition from `Vehicle`. The definition of `Car` is said to specialize the general `Vehicle` definition.

While `Vehicle` and `Car` collectively define the behavior by way of methods, the data in an instance would be things like the unique VIN of a specific car, etc.

And thus, classes, inheritance, and instantiation emerge.

Another key concept with classes is *polymorphism*, which describes the idea that a general behavior from a parent class can be overridden in a child class to give it more specifics. In fact, relative polymorphism lets us reference the base behavior from the overridden behavior.

Class theory strongly suggests that a parent class and a child class share the same method name for a certain behavior, so that the child overrides the parent (differentially). As we'll see later, doing so in your JavaScript code is opting into frustration and code brittleness.

"Class" Design Pattern

You may never have thought about classes as a design pattern, since it's most common to see discussion of popular OO design patterns, like *Iterator, Observer, Factory, Singleton*, etc. As presented this way, it's almost an assumption that OO classes are the lower-level mechanics by which we implement all (higher-level) design patterns, as if OO is a given foundation for *all* (proper) code.

Depending on your level of formal education in programming, you may have heard of *procedural programming* as a way of describing code that only consists of procedures (aka functions) calling other functions, without any higher abstractions. You may have been taught that classes were the *proper* way to transform procedural-style "spaghetti code" into well-formed, well-organized code.

Of course, if you have experience with *functional programming* (Monads, etc.), you know very well that classes are just one of several common design patterns. But for others, this may be the first time you've asked yourself if classes really are a fundamental foundation for code, or if they are an optional abstraction on top of code.

Some languages (like Java) don't give you the choice, so it's not very *optional* at all—everything's a class. Other languages like C/C++ or PHP give you both procedural and class-oriented syntaxes, and it's left more to the developer's choice which style or mixture of styles is appropriate.

JavaScript "Classes"

Where does JavaScript fall in this regard? JS has had *some* class-like syntactic elements (like `new` and `instanceof`) for quite a while, and more recently in ES6, some additions, like the `class` keyword (see Appendix A).

But does that mean JavaScript actually *has* classes? Plain and simple: **NO**.

Since classes are a design pattern, you *can*, with quite a bit of effort (as we'll see throughout the rest of this chapter), implement approximations for much of classical class functionality. JS tries to satisfy the extremely pervasive *desire* to design with classes by providing seemingly class-like syntax.

While we may have a syntax that looks like classes, it's as if JavaScript mechanics are fighting against you using the *class design pattern*, because behind the curtain, the mechanisms that you build on are operating quite differently. Syntactic sugar and (extremely widely used) JS "class" libraries go a long way toward hiding this reality from you, but sooner or later you will face the fact that the *classes* you have in other languages are not like the "classes" you're faking in JS.

What this boils down to is that classes are an optional pattern in software design, and you have the choice to use them in JavaScript or not. Since many developers have a strong affinity to class-oriented software design, we'll spend the rest of this chapter exploring what it takes to maintain the illusion of classes with what JS provides, and the pain points we experience.

Class Mechanics

In many class-oriented languages, the "standard library" provides a "stack" data structure (push, pop, etc.) as a Stack class. This class would have an internal set of variables that stores the data, and it would have a set of publicly accessible behaviors ("methods") provided by the class, which gives your code the ability to interact with the (hidden) data (adding and removing data, etc.).

But in such languages, you don't really operate directly on Stack (unless making a static class member reference, which is outside the scope of our discussion). The Stack class is merely an abstract explanation of what *any* "stack" should do, but it's not itself *a* "stack." You must instantiate the Stack class before you have a concrete data structure *thing* to operate against.

Building

The traditional metaphor for "class"- and "instance"-based thinking comes from building construction.

An architect plans out all the characteristics of a building: how wide, how tall, how many windows and in what locations, even what type of material to use for the walls and roof. She doesn't necessarily care, at this point, *where* the building will be built, nor does she care *how many* copies of that building will be built.

The architect also doesn't care very much about the contents of the building—the furniture, wallpaper, ceiling fans, etc.—only what type of structure they will be contained by.

The architectural blueprints are only *plans* for a building. They don't actually constitute a building where we can walk in and sit down. We need a builder for that task. A builder will take those plans and follow them, exactly, as he *builds* the building. In a very real sense, he is *copying* the intended characteristics from the plans to the physical building.

Once complete, the building is a physical instantiation of the blueprint plans, hopefully an essentially perfect *copy*. And then the builder can move to the open lot next door and do it all over again, creating yet another *copy*.

The relationship between the building and blueprint is indirect. You can examine a blueprint to understand how the building was structured, for any parts where direct inspection of the building itself was insufficient. But if you want to open a door, you have to go to the building itself—the blueprint merely has lines drawn on a page that *represent* where the door should be.

A class is a blueprint. To actually *get* an object we can interact with, we must build (aka *instantiate*) something from the class. The end result of such "construction" is an object, typically called an *instance*, which we can directly call methods on and access any public data properties from, as necessary.

This object is a *copy* of all the characteristics described by the class.

You likely wouldn't expect to walk into a building and find, framed and hanging on the wall, a copy of the blueprints used to plan the building, though the blueprints are probably on file with a public records office. Similarly, you don't generally use an object instance to directly access and manipulate its class, but it is usually possible to at least determine *which class* an object instance comes from.

It's more useful to consider the direct relationship of a class to an object instance, rather than any indirect relationship between an object instance and the class it came from. A class is instantiated into object form by a copy operation:

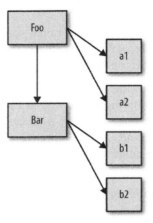

As you can see, the arrows move from left to right, and from top to bottom, which indicates the copy operations that occur, both conceptually and physically.

Constructor

Instances of classes are constructed by a special method of the class, usually of the same name as the class, called a *constructor*. This method's explicit job is to initialize any information (state) the instance will need.

For example, consider this loose pseudocode (invented syntax) for classes:

```
class CoolGuy {
    specialTrick = nothing

    CoolGuy( trick ) {
        specialTrick = trick
    }

    showOff() {
        output( "Here's my trick: ", specialTrick )
    }
}
```

To *make* a CoolGuy instance, we would call the class constructor:

```
Joe = new CoolGuy( "jumping rope" )

Joe.showOff() // Here's my trick: jumping rope
```

Notice that the CoolGuy class has a constructor CoolGuy(), which is actually what we call when we say new CoolGuy(..). We get an object back (an instance of our class) from the constructor, and we can call the method showOff(), which prints out that particular CoolGuy's special trick.

Obviously, jumping rope makes Joe a pretty cool guy.

The constructor of a class *belongs* to the class, and almost universally has the same name as the class. Also, constructors pretty much always need to be called with new to let the language engine know you want to construct a *new* class instance.

Class Inheritance

In class-oriented languages, not only can you define a class that can be instantiated itself, but you can define another class that inherits from the first class.

The second class is often said to be a "child class," whereas the first is the "parent class." These terms obviously come from the metaphor of parents and children, though the metaphors here are a bit stretched, as you'll see shortly.

When a parent has a biological child, the genetic characteristics of the parent are copied into the child. Obviously, in most biological reproduction systems, there are two parents who coequally contribute genes to the mix. But for the purposes of the metaphor, we'll assume just one parent.

Once the child exists, he is separate from the parent. The child was heavily influenced by the inheritance from his parent, but is unique and distinct. If a child ends up with red hair, that doesn't mean the parent's hair *was* or automatically *becomes* red.

In a similar way, once a child class is defined, it's separate and distinct from the parent class. The child class contains an initial copy of the behavior from the parent, but can then override any inherited behavior and even define new behavior.

It's important to remember that we're talking about parent and child classes, which aren't physical things. This is where the metaphor of parent and child gets a little confusing, because we actually should say that a parent class is like a parent's DNA and a child class is like a child's DNA. We have to make (aka instantiate) a person out of each set of DNA to actually have a physical person to have a conversation with.

Let's set aside biological parents and children, and look at inheritance through a slightly different lens: different types of vehicles. That's one of the most canonical (and often groan-worthy) metaphors to understand inheritance.

Let's revisit the Vehicle and Car discussion from earlier in this chapter. Consider this loose pseudocode (invented syntax) for inherited classes:

```
class Vehicle {
    engines = 1

    ignition() {
        output( "Turning on my engine." );
    }

    drive() {
        ignition();
        output( "Steering and moving forward!" )
    }
}

class Car inherits Vehicle {
    wheels = 4

    drive() {
        inherited:drive()
        output( "Rolling on all ", wheels, " wheels!" )
    }
}

class SpeedBoat inherits Vehicle {
    engines = 2

    ignition() {
        output( "Turning on my ", engines, " engines." )
    }

    pilot() {
        inherited:drive()
        output( "Speeding through the water with ease!" )
    }
}
```

For clarity and brevity, constructors for these classes have been omitted.

We define the Vehicle class to assume an engine, a way to turn on the ignition, and a way to drive around. But you wouldn't ever manufacture just a generic "vehicle," so it's really just an abstract concept at this point.

So then we define two specific kinds of vehicle: Car and SpeedBoat. They each inherit the general characteristics of Vehicle, but then they specialize the characteristics appropriately for each kind. A car needs four wheels, and a speedboat needs two engines, which means it needs extra attention to turn on the ignition of both engines.

Polymorphism

Car defines its own drive() method, which overrides the method of the same name it inherited from Vehicle. But then, Car's drive() method calls inherited:drive(), which indicates that Car can reference the original pre-overridden drive() it inherited. SpeedBoat's pilot() method also makes a reference to its inherited copy of drive().

This technique is called *polymorphism*, or *virtual polymorphism*. More specifically to our current point, we'll call it *relative polymorphism*.

Polymorphism is a much broader topic than we will exhaust here, but our current "relative" semantics refer to one particular aspect: the idea that any method can reference another method (of the same or different name) at a higher level of the inheritance hierarchy. We say "relative" because we don't absolutely define which inheritance level (aka class) we want to access, but rather relatively reference it by essentially saying "look one level up."

In many languages, the keyword super is used, in place of this example's inherited:, which leans on the idea that a "superclass" is the parent/ancestor of the current class.

Another aspect of polymorphism is that a method name can have multiple definitions at different levels of the inheritance chain, and these definitions are automatically selected as appropriate when resolving which methods are being called.

We see two occurrences of that behavior in our previous example: `drive()` is defined in both `Vehicle` and `Car`, and `ignition()` is defined in both `Vehicle` and `SpeedBoat`.

 Another thing that traditional class-oriented languages give you via `super` is a direct way for the constructor of a child class to reference the constructor of its parent class. This is largely true because with real classes, the constructor belongs to the class. However, in JS, it's the reverse—it's actually more appropriate to think of the "class" belonging to the constructor (the `Foo.prototype...` type references). Since in JS the relationship between child and parent exists only between the two `.prototype` objects of the respective constructors, the constructors themselves are not directly related, and thus there's no simple way to relatively reference one from the other (see Appendix A on the ES6 `class`, which "solves" this with `super`).

An interesting implication of polymorphism can be seen specifically with `ignition()`. Inside `pilot()`, a relative-polymorphic reference is made to (the inherited) `Vehicle`'s version of `drive()`. But that `drive()` references an `ignition()` method just by name (no relative reference).

Which version of `ignition()` will the language engine use, the one from `Vehicle` or the one from `SpeedBoat`? It uses the `SpeedBoat` version of `ignition()`. If you *were* to instantiate the `Vehicle` class itself, and then call its `drive()`, the language engine would instead just use `Vehicle`'s `ignition()` method definition.

Put another way, the definition for the method `ignition()` *polymorphs* (changes) depending on which class (level of inheritance) you are referencing an instance of.

This may seem like overly deep academic detail. But understanding these details is necessary to properly contrast similar (but distinct) behaviors in JavaScript's `[[Prototype]]` mechanism.

When classes are inherited, there is a way for the classes themselves (not the object instances created from them!) to *relatively* reference the class inherited from, and this relative reference is usually called `super`.

Remember this figure from earlier?

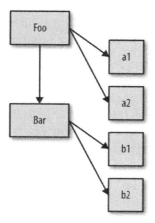

Notice how for both instantiation (a1, a2, b1, and b2) *and* inheritance (Bar), the arrows indicate a copy operation.

Conceptually, it would seem a child class Bar can access behavior in its parent class Foo using a relative polymorphic reference (aka super). However, in reality, the child class is merely given a copy of the inherited behavior from its parent class. If the child "overrides" a method it inherits, both the original and overridden verions of the method are actually maintained, so that they are both accessible.

Don't let polymorphism confuse you into thinking a child class is linked to its parent class. A child class instead gets a copy of what it needs from the parent class. Class inheritance implies copies.

Multiple Inheritance

Recall our earlier discussion of parent(s) and children and DNA? We said that the metaphor was a bit weird because biologically most off-spring come from two parents. If a class could inherit from two other classes, it would more closely fit the parent/child metaphor.

Some class-oriented languages allow you to specify more than one "parent" class to "inherit" from. Multiple inheritance means that each parent class definition is copied into the child class.

On the surface, this seems like a powerful addition to class orientation, giving us the ability to compose more functionality together. However, there are certainly some complicating questions that arise. If both parent classes provide a method called drive(), which version would a drive() reference in the child resolve to? Would you always have to manually specify which parent's drive() you meant, thus losing some of the gracefulness of polymorphic inheritance?

There's another variation, the so-called *diamond problem*, which refers to the scenario where a child class D inherits from two parent classes (B and C), and each of those in turn inherits from a common A parent. If A provides a method drive(), and both B and C override (polymorph) that method, when D references drive(), which version should it use (B:drive() or C:drive())?

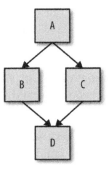

These complications go much deeper than this quick glance. We address them here only so we can contrast with how JavaScript's mechanisms work.

JavaScript is simpler: it does not provide a native mechanism for "multiple inheritance." Many see this is a good thing, because the complexity savings more than make up for the "reduced" functionality. But this doesn't stop developers from trying to fake it in various ways, as we'll see next.

Mixins

JavaScript's object mechanism does not *automatically* perform copy behavior when you inherit or instantiate. Plainly, there are no "classes" in JavaScript to instantiate, only objects. And objects don't get copied to other objects, they get *linked together* (more on that in Chapter 5).

Since observed class behaviors in other languages imply copies, let's examine how JS developers fake the *missing* copy behavior of classes in JavaScript: *mixins*. We'll look at two types of mixin: *explicit* and *implicit*.

Explicit Mixins

Let's again revisit our Vehicle and Car example from before. Since JavaScript will not automatically copy behavior from Vehicle to Car, we can instead create a utility that manually copies. Such a utility is often called extend(..) by many libraries/frameworks, but we will call it mixin(..) here for illustrative purposes:

```
// vastly simplified `mixin(..)` example:
function mixin( sourceObj, targetObj ) {
    for (var key in sourceObj) {
        // only copy if not already present
        if (!(key in targetObj)) {
            targetObj[key] = sourceObj[key];
        }
    }

    return targetObj;
}

var Vehicle = {
    engines: 1,

    ignition: function() {
        console.log( "Turning on my engine." );
    },

    drive: function() {
        this.ignition();
        console.log( "Steering and moving forward!" );
    }
};

var Car = mixin( Vehicle, {
    wheels: 4,

    drive: function() {
        Vehicle.drive.call( this );
        console.log(
            "Rolling on all " + this.wheels + " wheels!"
        );
    }
} );
```

Subtly but importantly, we're not dealing with classes anymore, because there are no classes in JavaScript. Vehicle and Car are just objects that we make copies from and to, respectively.

Car now has a copy of the properties and functions from Vehicle. Technically, functions are not actually duplicated, but rather *references* to the functions are copied. So, Car now has a property called ignition, which is a copied reference to the ignition() function, as well as a property called engines with the copied value of 1 from Vehicle.

Car *already* had a drive property (function), so that property reference was not overridden (see the if statement in mixin(..) earlier).

Polymorphism revisited

Let's examine this statement: Vehicle.drive.call(this). This is what I call *explicit pseudopolymorphism*. Recall in our previous pseudocode this line was inherited:drive(), which we called *relative polymorphism*.

JavaScript does not have (prior to ES6; see Appendix A) a facility for relative polymorphism. So, because both Car and Vehicle had a function of the same name, drive(), to distinguish a call to one or the other, we must make an absolute (not relative) reference. We explicitly specify the Vehicle object by name and call the drive() function on it.

But if we said Vehicle.drive(), the this binding for that function call would be the Vehicle object instead of the Car object (see Chapter 2), which is not what we want. So, instead we use .call(this) (Chapter 2) to ensure that drive() is executed in the context of the Car object.

If the function name identifier for Car.drive() hadn't overlapped with (aka "shadowed"; see Chapter 5) Vehi cle.drive(), we wouldn't have been exercising method polymorphism. So, a reference to Vehicle.drive() would have been copied over by the mixin(..) call, and we could have accessed directly with this.drive(). The chosen identifier overlap shadowing is why we have to use the more complex explicit pseudopolymorphism approach.

In class-oriented languages, which have relative polymorphism, the linkage between Car and Vehicle is established once, at the top of the class definition, which makes for only one place to maintain such relationships.

But because of JavaScript's peculiarities, explicit pseudopolymorphism (because of shadowing!) creates brittle manual/explicit linkage in every single function where you need such a (pseudo)polymorphic reference. This can significantly increase the maintenance cost. Moreover, while explicit pseudopolymorphism can emulate the behavior of multiple inheritance, it only increases the complexity and brittleness.

The result of such approaches is usually more complex, harder-to-read, *and* harder-to-maintain code. Explicit pseudopolymorphism should be avoided wherever possible, because the cost outweighs the benefit in most respects.

Mixing copies

Recall the mixin(..) utility from earlier:

```
// vastly simplified `mixin()` example:
function mixin( sourceObj, targetObj ) {
    for (var key in sourceObj) {
        // only copy if not already present
        if (!(key in targetObj)) {
            targetObj[key] = sourceObj[key];
        }
    }

    return targetObj;
}
```

Now, let's examine how mixin(..) works. It iterates over the properties of sourceObj (Vehicle, in our example), and if there's no matching property of that name in targetObj (Car, in our example), it makes a copy. Since we're making the copy after the initial object exists, we are careful to not copy over a target property.

If we made the copies first, before specifying the Car-specific contents, we could omit this check against targetObj, but that's a little more clunky and less efficient, so it's generally less preferred:

```
// alternate mixin, less "safe" to overwrites
function mixin( sourceObj, targetObj ) {
    for (var key in sourceObj) {
        targetObj[key] = sourceObj[key];
    }

    return targetObj;
}

var Vehicle = {
    // ...
};

// first, create an empty object with
// Vehicle's stuff copied in
var Car = mixin( Vehicle, { } );

// now copy the intended contents into Car
mixin( {
    wheels: 4,

    drive: function() {
        // ...
    }
}, Car );
```

With either approach, we have explicitly copied the nonoverlapping contents of Vehicle into Car. The name "mixin" comes from an alternate way of explaining the task: Car has Vehicle's contents mixed in, just like you mix in chocolate chips into your favorite cookie dough.

As a result of the copy operation, Car will operate somewhat separately from Vehicle. If you add a property onto Car, it will not affect Vehicle, and vice versa.

 A few minor details have been skimmed over here. There are still some subtle ways the two objects can "affect" each other even after copying, such as if they both share a reference to a common object (such as an array).

Since the two objects also share references to their common functions, that means that even manual copying of functions (aka mixins) from one object to another doesn't actually emulate the real duplication from class to instance that occurs in class-oriented languages.

JavaScript functions can't really be duplicated (in a standard, reliable way), so what you end up with instead is a *duplicated reference* to the same shared function object (functions are objects; see Chapter 3). If you modified one of the shared function objects (like `ignition()`) by adding properties on top of it, for instance, both `Vehicle` and `Car` would be "affected" via the shared reference.

Explicit mixins are a fine mechanism in JavaScript. But they appear more powerful than they really are. Not much benefit is *actually* derived from copying a property from one object to another, as opposed to just defining the properties twice, once on each object. And that's especially true given the function-object reference nuance we just mentioned.

If you explicitly mix in two or more objects into your target object, you can partially emulate the behavior of multiple inheritance, but there's no direct way to handle collisions if the same method or property is being copied from more than one source. Some developers/libraries have come up with "late binding" techniques and other exotic workarounds, but fundamentally, these "tricks" are *usually* more effort (with less performance!) than the payoff.

Take care only to use explicit mixins where it actually helps make more readable code, and avoid the pattern if you find it making code that's harder to trace, or if you find it creates unnecessary or unwieldy dependencies between objects.

If it starts to get *harder* to properly use mixins than before you used them, you should probably stop using mixins. In fact, if you have to use a complex library/utility to work out all these details, it might be a sign that you're going about it the harder way, perhaps unnecessarily. In Chapter 6, we'll try to distill a simpler way that accomplishes the desired outcomes without all the fuss.

Parasitic inheritance

A variation on this explicit mixin pattern, which is both in some ways explicit and in other ways implicit, is called "parasitic inheritance," popularized mainly by Douglas Crockford.

Here's how it can work:

```javascript
// "Traditional JS Class" `Vehicle`
function Vehicle() {
    this.engines = 1;
}
Vehicle.prototype.ignition = function() {
    console.log( "Turning on my engine." );
};
Vehicle.prototype.drive = function() {
    this.ignition();
    console.log( "Steering and moving forward!" );
};

// "Parasitic Class" `Car`
function Car() {
    // first, `car` is a `Vehicle`
    var car = new Vehicle();

    // now, let's modify our `car` to specialize it
    car.wheels = 4;

    // save a privileged reference to `Vehicle::drive()`
    var vehDrive = car.drive;

    // override `Vehicle::drive()`
    car.drive = function() {
        vehDrive.call( this );
        console.log(
            "Rolling on all " + this.wheels + " wheels!"
        );
    };

    return car;
}

var myCar = new Car();

myCar.drive();
// Turning on my engine.
// Steering and moving forward!
// Rolling on all 4 wheels!
```

As you can see, we initially make a copy of the definition from the Vehicle parent class (object), then mix in our child class (object) definition (preserving privileged parent-class references as needed), and pass off this composed object car as our child instance.

When we call new Car(), a new object is created and referenced by Car's this reference (see Chapter 2). But since we don't use that object, and instead return our own car object, the initially created object is just discarded. So, Car() could be called without the new keyword, and the functionality just described would be identical, but without the wasted object creation/garbage collection.

Implicit Mixins

Implicit mixins are closely related to explicit pseudopolymorphism, as explained previously. As such, they come with the same caveats and warnings.

Consider this code:

```
var Something = {
    cool: function() {
        this.greeting = "Hello World";
        this.count = this.count ? this.count + 1 : 1;
    }
};

Something.cool();
Something.greeting; // "Hello World"
Something.count; // 1

var Another = {
    cool: function() {
        // implicit mixin of `Something` to `Another`
        Something.cool.call( this );
    }
};

Another.cool();
Another.greeting; // "Hello World"
Another.count; // 1 (not shared state with `Something`)
```

With Something.cool.call(this), which can happen either in a constructor call (most common) or in a method call (shown here), we essentially "borrow" the function Something.cool() and call it in the context of Another (via its this binding; see Chapter 2) instead of Something. The end result is that the assignments that Something.cool() makes are applied against the Another object rather than the Something object.

So, it is said that we "mixed in" `Something`'s behavior with (or into) `Another`.

While this sort of technique seems to take useful advantage of `this` rebinding functionality, it's a brittle `Something.cool.call( this )` call, which cannot be made into a relative (and thus more flexible) reference, that you should heed with caution. Generally, avoid such constructs wherever possible to keep cleaner and more maintainable code.

Review

Classes are a design pattern. Many languages provide syntax that enables natural class-oriented software design. JS also has a similar syntax, but it behaves very differently from what you're used to with classes in those other languages.

Classes mean copies.

When traditional classes are instantiated, a copy of behavior from class to instance occurs. When classes are inherited, a copy of behavior from parent to child also occurs.

Polymorphism (having different functions at multiple levels of an inheritance chain with the same name) may seem like it implies a referential relative link from child back to parent, but it's still just a result of copy behavior.

JavaScript does not automatically create copies (as classes imply) between objects.

The mixin pattern (both explicit and implicit) is often used to *sort of* emulate class copy behavior, but this usually leads to ugly and brittle syntax like explicit pseudopolymorphism (`OtherObj.method Name.call(this, ...)`), which often results in code that is harder to understand and maintain.

Explicit mixins are also not exactly the same as class-copy behavior, since objects (and functions!) only have shared references duplicated, not the objects/functions themselves. Not paying attention to such nuance is the source of a variety of gotchas.

In general, faking classes in JS often sets more landmines for future coding than solving present *real* problems.

CHAPTER 5

Prototypes

In Chapters 3 and 4, we mentioned the [[Prototype]] chain several times, but haven't said what exactly it is. We will now examine prototypes in detail.

 All of the attempts to emulate class-copy behavior described previously in Chapter 4, labeled as variations of mixins, completely circumvent the [[Prototype]] chain mechanism we examine here in this chapter.

[[Prototype]]

Objects in JavaScript have an internal property, denoted in the specification as [[Prototype]], which is simply a reference to another object. Almost all objects are given a non-null value for this property, at the time of their creation.

Note: we will see shortly that it *is* possible for an object to have an empty [[Prototype]] linkage, though this is somewhat less common.

Consider:

```
var myObject = {
    a: 2
};

myObject.a; // 2
```

What is the [[Prototype]] reference used for? In Chapter 3, we examined the [[Get]] operation that is invoked when you reference a property on an object, such as `myObject.a`. For that default `[[Get]]` operation, the first step is to check if the object itself has a property a on it, and if so, it's used.

ES6 Proxies are outside of our discussion scope in this book (they will be covered in a later book in the series), but everything we discuss here about normal `[[Get]]` and `[[Put]]` behavior does not apply if a `Proxy` is involved.

But it's what happens if a *isn't* present on `myObject` that brings our attention now to the `[[Prototype]]` link of the object.

The default `[[Get]]` operation proceeds to follow the `[[Prototype]]` link of the object if it cannot find the requested property on the object directly:

```
var anotherObject = {
    a: 2
};

// create an object linked to `anotherObject`
var myObject = Object.create( anotherObject );

myObject.a; // 2
```

We will explain what `Object.create(..)` does, and how it operates, shortly. For now, just assume it creates an object with the `[[Prototype]]` linkage we're examining to the object specified.

So, we have `myObject` that is now `[[Prototype]]` linked to `another Object`. Clearly `myObject.a` doesn't actually exist, but nevertheless, the property access succeeds (being found on `anotherObject` instead) and indeed finds the value 2.

But, if a weren't found on `anotherObject` either, its `[[Prototype]]` chain, if nonempty, is again consulted and followed.

This process continues until either a matching property name is found, or the `[[Prototype]]` chain ends. If no matching property is *ever* found by the end of the chain, the return result from the `[[Get]]` operation is `undefined`.

Similar to this [[Prototype]] chain lookup process, if you use a for..in loop to iterate over an object, any property that can be reached via its chain (and is also enumerable—see Chapter 3) will be enumerated. If you use the in operator to test for the existence of a property on an object, in will check the entire chain of the object (regardless of *enumerability*):

```
var anotherObject = {
    a: 2
};

// create an object linked to `anotherObject`
var myObject = Object.create( anotherObject );

for (var k in myObject) {
    console.log("found: " + k);
}
// found: a

("a" in myObject); // true
```

So, the [[Prototype]] chain is consulted, one link at a time, when you perform property lookups in various fashions. The lookup stops once the property is found or the chain ends.

Object.prototype

But *where* exactly does the [[Prototype]] chain "end"?

The top end of every *normal* [[Prototype]] chain is the built-in Object.prototype. This object includes a variety of common utilities used all over JS, because all normal (built-in, not host-specific extension) objects in JavaScript "descend from" (aka have at the top of their [[Prototype]] chain) the Object.prototype object.

Some utilities found here you may be familiar with include .toString() and .valueOf(). In Chapter 3, we introduced another: .hasOwnProperty(..). And yet another function on Object.prototype you may not be familiar with is .isPrototypeOf(..), which we'll address later in this chapter.

Setting and Shadowing Properties

Back in Chapter 3, we mentioned that setting properties on an object was more nuanced than just adding a new property to the object or changing an existing property's value. We will now revisit this situation more completely:

```
myObject.foo = "bar";
```

If the myObject object already has a normal data accessor property called foo directly present on it, the assignment is as simple as changing the value of the existing property.

If foo is not already present directly on myObject, the [[Prototype]] chain is traversed, just like for the [[Get]] operation. If foo is not found anywhere in the chain, the property foo is added directly to myObject with the specified value, as expected.

However, if foo is already present somewhere higher in the chain, nuanced (and perhaps surprising) behavior can occur with the myObject.foo = "bar" assignment. We'll examine that more in just a moment.

If the property name foo ends up both on myObject itself and at a higher level of the [[Prototype]] chain that starts at myObject, this is called *shadowing*. The foo property directly on myObject *shadows* any foo property that appears higher in the chain, because the myObject.foo lookup would always find the foo property that's lowest in the chain.

As we just hinted, shadowing foo on myObject is not as simple as it may seem. We will now examine three scenarios for the myObject.foo = "bar" assignment when foo is not already on myObject directly, but *is* at a higher level of myObject's [[Prototype]] chain:

1. If a normal data accessor (see Chapter 3) property named foo is found anywhere higher on the [[Prototype]] chain, and it's not marked as read-only (writable:false), then a new property called foo is added directly to myObject, resulting in a *shadowed property*.

2. If a foo is found higher on the [[Prototype]] chain, but it's marked as read-only (writable:false), then both the setting of that existing property as well as the creation of the shadowed property on myObject are disallowed. If the code is running in strict mode, an error will be thrown. Otherwise, the setting of the property value will silently be ignored. Either way, no shadowing occurs.

3. If a `foo` is found higher on the `[[Prototype]]` chain and it's a setter (see Chapter 3), then the setter will always be called. No `foo` will be added to (aka shadowed on) `myObject`, nor will the `foo` setter be redefined.

Most developers assume that assignment of a property (`[[Put]]`) will always result in shadowing if the property already exists higher on the `[[Prototype]]` chain, but as you can see, that's only true in one of the three situations just described (case 1).

If you want to shadow `foo` in cases 2 and 3, you cannot use = assignment, but must instead use `Object.defineProperty(..)` (see Chapter 3) to add `foo` to `myObject`.

Case 2 may be the most surprising of the three. The presence of a *read-only* property prevents a property of the same name from being implicitly created (shadowed) at a lower level of a `[[Prototype]]` chain. The reason for this restriction is primarily to reinforce the illusion of class-inherited properties. If you think of the `foo` at a higher level of the chain as having been inherited (copied down) to `myObject`, then it makes sense to enforce the nonwritable nature of that `foo` property on `my Object`. If you however separate the illusion from the fact, and recognize that no such inheritance copying *actually* occured (see Chapters 4 and 5), it's a little unnatural that `myObject` would be prevented from having a `foo` property just because some other object had a nonwritable `foo` on it. It's even stranger that this restriction only applies to = assignment, but is not enforced when using `Object.defineProperty(..)`.

Shadowing methods leads to ugly explicit pseudopolymorphism (see Chapter 4) if you need to delegate between them. Usually, shadowing is more complicated and nuanced than it's worth, so you should try to avoid it if possible. See Chapter 6 for an alternative design pattern, which among other things, discourages shadowing in favor of cleaner alternatives.

Shadowing can even occur implicitly in subtle ways, so care must be taken if trying to avoid it. Consider:

```
var anotherObject = {
    a: 2
};
```

```
var myObject = Object.create( anotherObject );

anotherObject.a; // 2
myObject.a; // 2

anotherObject.hasOwnProperty( "a" ); // true
myObject.hasOwnProperty( "a" ); // false

myObject.a++; // oops, implicit shadowing!

anotherObject.a; // 2
myObject.a; // 3

myObject.hasOwnProperty( "a" ); // true
```

Though it may appear that myObject.a++ should (via delegation) look up and just increment the anotherObject.a property itself *in place*, instead the ++ operation corresponds to myObject.a = myObject.a + 1. The result is [[Get]] looking up a property via [[Prototype]] to get the current value 2 from anotherObject.a, incrementing the value by one, then [[Put]] assigning the 3 value to a new shadowed property a on myObject. Oops!

Be very careful when dealing with delegated properties that you modify. If you wanted to increment anotherObject.a, the only proper way is anotherObject.a++.

"Class"

At this point, you might be wondering: *Why* does one object need to link to another object? What's the real benefit? That is a very appropriate question to ask, but we must first understand what [[Prototype]] is *not* before we can fully understand and appreciate what it *is* and how it's useful.

As we explained in Chapter 4, in JavaScript, there are no abstract patterns/blueprints for objects called classes as there are in class-oriented languages. JavaScript *just* has objects.

In fact, JavaScript is almost unique among languages as perhaps the only language with the right to use the label "object-oriented," because it's one of a very short list of languages where an object can be created directly, without a class at all.

In JavaScript, classes can't (being that they don't exist!) describe what an object can do. The object defines its own behavior directly. There's *just* the object.

"Class" Functions

There's a peculiar kind of behavior in JavaScript that has been shamelessly abused for years to *hack* something that *looks* like classes. We'll examine this approach in detail.

The peculiar "sort-of class" behavior hinges on a strange characteristic of functions: all functions by default get a public, nonenumerable (see Chapter 3) property on them called `prototype`, which points at an otherwise arbitrary object:

```
function Foo() {
    // ...
}

Foo.prototype; // { }
```

This object is often called *Foo's prototype*, because we access it via an unfortunately named `Foo.prototype` property reference. However, that terminology is hopelessly destined to lead us into confusion, as we'll see shortly. Instead, I will call it "the object formerly known as Foo's prototype." Just kidding. How about "the object arbitrarily labeled *Foo dot prototype*"?

Whatever we call it, what exactly is this object?

The most direct way to explain it is that each object created from calling new `Foo()` (see Chapter 2) will end up (somewhat arbitrarily) `[[Prototype]]`-linked to this "Foo dot prototype" object.

Let's illustrate:

```
function Foo() {
    // ...
}

var a = new Foo();

Object.getPrototypeOf( a ) === Foo.prototype; // true
```

When a is created by calling new Foo( ), one of the things that happens (see Chapter 2 for all *four* steps) is that a gets an internal [[Prototype]] link to the object that Foo.prototype is pointing at.

Stop for a moment and ponder the implications of that statement.

In class-oriented languages, multiple *copies* (aka instances) of a class can be made, like stamping something out from a mold. As we saw in Chapter 4, this happens because the process of instantiating (or inheriting from) a class means, "copy the behavior plan from that class into a physical object," and this is done again for each new instance.

But in JavaScript, there are no such copy actions performed. You don't create multiple instances of a class. You can create multiple objects that are [[Prototype]]-linked to a common object. But by default, no copying occurs, and thus these objects don't end up totally separate and disconnected from each other, but rather, quite *linked*.

new Foo( ) results in a new object (we called it a), and *that* new object a is internally [[Prototype]]-linked to the Foo.prototype object.

We end up with two objects, linked to each other. That's it. We didn't instantiate a class. We certainly didn't do any copying of behavior from a "class" into a concrete object. We just caused two objects to be linked to each other.

In fact, the secret, which eludes most JS developers, is that the new Foo( ) function calling had really almost nothing *direct* to do with the process of creating the link. It was sort of an accidental side effect. new Foo( ) is an indirect, roundabout way to end up with what we want: a new object linked to another object.

Can we get what we want in a more *direct* way? Yes! The hero is Object.create(..). But we'll get to that in a little bit.

What's in a name?

In JavaScript, we don't make *copies* from one object ("class") to another ("instance"). We make *links* between objects. For the [[Prototype]] mechanism, visually, the arrows move from right to left, and from bottom to top:

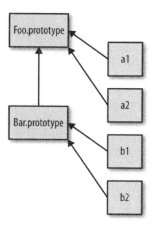

This mechanism is often called *prototypal inheritance* (we'll explore the code in detail shortly), which is commonly said to be the dynamic-language version of classical inheritance. It's an attempt to piggyback on the common understanding of what "inheritance" means in the class-oriented world, but *tweak* (read: pave over) the understood semantics, to fit dynamic scripting.

The word "inheritance" has a very strong meaning (see Chapter 4), with plenty of mental precedent. Merely adding "prototypal" in front to distinguish the *actually nearly opposite* behavior in JavaScript has left in its wake nearly two decades of miry confusion.

I like to say that sticking "prototypal" in front of "inheritance" to drastically reverse its actual meaning is like holding an orange in one hand, an apple in the other, and insisting on calling the apple a "red orange." No matter what confusing label I put in front of it, that doesn't change the *fact* that one fruit is an apple and the other is an orange.

The better approach is to plainly call an apple an apple—to use the most accurate and direct terminology. That makes it easier to understand both their similarities and their many differences, because we all have a simple, shared understanding of what "apple" means.

Because of the confusion and conflation of terms, I believe the label "prototypal inheritance" itself (and trying to misapply all its associated class-orientation terminology, like "class," "constructor," "instance," "polymorphism," etc.) has done more harm than good in explaining how JavaScript's mechanism *really* works.

Inheritance implies a *copy* operation, and JavaScript doesn't copy object properties (natively, by default). Instead, JS creates a link between two objects, where one object can essentially *delegate* property/function access to another object. *Delegation* (see Chapter 6) is a much more accurate term for JavaScript's object-linking mechanism.

Another term that is sometimes thrown around in JavaScript is *differential inheritance*. The idea here is that we describe an object's behavior in terms of what is *different* from a more general descriptor. For example, you explain that a car is a kind of vehicle, but one that has exactly four wheels, rather than redescribing all the specifics of what makes up a general vehicle (engine, etc.).

If you try to think of any given object in JS as the sum total of all behavior that is *available* via delegation, and in your mind you flatten all that behavior into one tangible *thing*, then you can (sorta) see how differential inheritance might fit.

But just like with prototypal inheritance, differential inheritance pretends that your mental model is more important than what is physcially happening in the language. It overlooks the fact that object B is not actually differentially constructed, but is instead built with specific characteristics defined, alongside "holes" where nothing is defined. It is in these "holes" (gaps in, or lack of, definition) that delegation *can* take over and, on the fly, "fill them in" with delegated behavior.

The object is not, by native default, flattened into the single differential object, through copying, that the mental model of differential inheritance implies. As such, differential inheritance is just not as natural a fit for describing how JavaScript's [[Prototype]] mechanism actually works.

You *can choose* to prefer the differential inheritance terminology and mental model, as a matter of taste, but there's no denying the fact that it *only* fits the mental acrobatics in your mind, not the physical behavior in the engine.

"Constructors"

Let's go back to some earlier code:

```
function Foo() {
    // ...
}

var a = new Foo();
```

What exactly leads us to think Foo is a "class"?

For one, we see the use of the new keyword, just as we see in class-oriented languages when they construct class instances. For another, it appears that we are in fact executing a *constructor* method of a class, because Foo() is actually a method that gets called, just like how a real class's constructor gets called when you instantiate that class.

To further the confusion of "constructor" semantics, the arbitrarily labeled Foo.prototype object has another trick up its sleeve. Consider this code:

```
function Foo() {
    // ...
}

Foo.prototype.constructor === Foo; // true

var a = new Foo();
a.constructor === Foo; // true
```

The Foo.prototype object by default (at declaration-time on line 1 of the snippet!) gets a public, nonenumerable (see Chapter 3) property called .constructor, and this property is a reference back to the function (Foo in this case) that the object is associated with. Moreover, we see that object a created by the "constructor" call new Foo() *seems* to also have a property on it called .constructor, which similarly points to "the function which created it."

 This is not actually true. a has no .constructor property on it, and though a.constructor does in fact resolve to the Foo function, "constructor" does not actually mean "was constructed by," as it appears. We'll explain this strangeness shortly.

Oh, yeah, also...by convention in the JavaScript world, a "class" is named with a capital letter, so the fact that it's Foo instead of foo is a strong clue that we intend it to be a "class." That's totally obvious to you, right!?

This convention is so strong that many JS linters actually *complain* if you call new on a method with a lowercase name, or if we don't call new on a function that happens to start with a capital letter. It sort of boggles the mind that we struggle so much to get (fake) "class orientation" *right* in JavaScript that we create linter rules to ensure we use capital letters, even though the capital letter doesn't mean anything at all to the JS engine.

Constructor or call?

In the previous snippet, it's tempting to think that Foo is a constructor, because we call it with new and we observe that it "constructs" an object.

In reality, Foo is no more a "constructor" than any other function in your program. Functions themselves are *not* constructors. However, when you put the new keyword in front of a normal function call, that makes that function call a "constructor call." In fact, new sort of hijacks any normal function and calls it in a fashion that constructs an object, in addition to whatever else it was going to do.

For example:

```
function NothingSpecial() {
    console.log( "Don't mind me!" );
}

var a = new NothingSpecial();
// "Don't mind me!"

a; // {}
```

NothingSpecial is just a plain old normal function, but when called with new, it *constructs* an object, almost as a side effect, which we happen to assign to a. The call was a *constructor call*, but NothingSpecial is not, in and of itself, a *constructor*.

In other words, in JavaScript, it's most appropriate to say that a "constructor" is any function called with the new keyword in front of it.

Functions aren't constructors, but function calls are "constructor calls" if and only if new is used.

Mechanics

Are *those* the only common triggers for ill-fated "class" discussions in JavaScript?

Not quite. JS developers have strived to simulate as much as they can of class orientation:

```
function Foo(name) {
    this.name = name;
}

Foo.prototype.myName = function() {
    return this.name;
};

var a = new Foo( "a" );
var b = new Foo( "b" );

a.myName(); // "a"
b.myName(); // "b"
```

This snippet shows two additional "class orientation" tricks in play:

1. this.name = name adds the .name property onto each object (a and b, respectively; see Chapter 2 about this binding), similar to how class instances encapsulate data values.

2. Foo.prototype.myName = ... is perhaps the more interesting technique; this adds a property (function) to the Foo.prototype object. Now, a.myName() works, but perhaps surprisingly. How?

In the previous snippet, it's strongly tempting to think that when a and b are created, the properties/functions on the Foo.prototype object are *copied* over to each of the a and b objects. However, that's not what happens.

At the beginning of this chapter, we explained the [[Prototype]] link, and how it provides the fallback lookup steps if a property reference isn't found directly on an object, as part of the default [[Get]] algorithm.

So, by virtue of how they are created, a and b each end up with an internal [[Prototype]] linkage to Foo.prototype. When myName is not found on a or b, respectively, it's instead found (through delegation; see Chapter 6) on Foo.prototype.

"Constructor" redux

Recall the discussion from earlier about the `.constructor` property, and how it *seems* like `a.constructor === Foo` being true means that `a` has an actual `.constructor` property on it, pointing at `Foo`? Not correct.

This is just unfortunate confusion. In actuality, the `.constructor` reference is also delegated up to `Foo.prototype`, which happens to, by default, have a `.constructor` that points at `Foo`.

It *seems* awfully convenient that an object `a` "constructed by" `Foo` would have access to a `.constructor` property that points to `Foo`. But that's nothing more than a false sense of security. It's a happy accident, almost tangentially, that `a.constructor` *happens* to point at `Foo` via this default `[[Prototype]]` delegation. There are actually several ways that the ill-fated assumption of `.constructor` meaning "was constructed by" can come back to bite you.

For one, the `.constructor` property on `Foo.prototype` is only there by default on the object created when `Foo` the function is declared. If you create a new object, and replace a function's default `.prototype` object reference, the new object will not by default magically get a `.constructor` on it.

Consider:

```
function Foo() { /* .. */ }

Foo.prototype = { /* .. */ }; // create a new prototype object

var a1 = new Foo();
a1.constructor === Foo; // false!
a1.constructor === Object; // true!
```

`Object(..)` didn't "construct" `a1`, did it? It sure seems like `Foo()` "constructed" it. Most developers think of `Foo()` as doing the construction, but where everything falls apart is when you think "constructor" means "was constructed by," because by that reasoning, `a1.constructor` should be `Foo`, but it isn't!

What's happening? `a1` has no `.constructor` property, so it delegates up the `[[Prototype]]` chain to `Foo.prototype`. But that object doesn't have a `.constructor` either (like the default `Foo.prototype` object would have had!), so it keeps delegating, this time up to `Object.prototype`, the top of the delegation chain. *That* object indeed has a `.constructor` on it, which points to the built-in `Object(..)` function.

Misconception: busted.

Of course, you can add `.constructor` back to the `Foo.prototype` object, but this takes manual work, especially if you want to match native behavior and have it be nonenumerable (see Chapter 3).

For example:

```
function Foo() { /* .. */ }

Foo.prototype = { /* .. */ }; // create a new prototype object

// Need to properly "fix" the missing `.constructor`
// property on the new object serving as `Foo.prototype`.
// See Chapter 3 for `defineProperty(..)`.
Object.defineProperty( Foo.prototype, "constructor" , {
    enumerable: false,
    writable: true,
    configurable: true,
    value: Foo      // point `.constructor` at `Foo`
} );
```

That's a lot of manual work to fix `.constructor`. Moreover, all we're really doing is perpetuating the misconception that "constructor" means "was constructed by." That's an *expensive* illusion.

The fact is, `.constructor` on an object arbitrarily points, by default, at a function that, reciprocally, has a reference back to the object—a reference that it calls `.prototype`. The words "constructor" and "prototype" only have a loose default meaning that might or might not hold true later. The best thing to do is remind yourself that "constructor does not mean constructed by."

`.constructor` is not a magic immutable property. It *is* nonenumerable (see previous snippet), but its value is writable (can be changed), and moreover, you can add or overwrite (intentionally or accidentally) a property of the name `constructor` on any object in any `[[Prototype]]` chain, with any value you see fit.

By virtue of how the `[[Get]]` algorithm traverses the `[[Prototype]]` chain, a `.constructor` property reference found anywhere may resolve quite differently than you'd expect.

See how arbitrary its meaning actually is?

The result? Some arbitrary object-property reference like `a1.con structor` cannot actually be *trusted* to be the assumed default function reference. Moreover, as we'll see shortly, just by simple omission, `a1.constructor` can even end up pointing somewhere quite surprising and insensible.

`a1.constructor` is extremely unreliable, and it's an unsafe reference to rely upon in your code. Generally, such references should be avoided where possible.

(Prototypal) Inheritance

We've seen some approximations of class mechanics as typically hacked into JavaScript programs. But JavaScript classes would be rather hollow if we didn't have an approximation of "inheritance."

Actually, we've already seen the mechanism commonly called prototypal inheritance at work when a was able to "inherit from" `Foo.pro totype`, and thus get access to the `myName()` function. But we traditionally think of inheritance as being a relationship between two classes, rather than between class and instance:

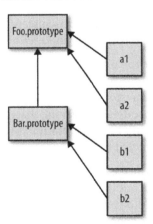

Recall this figure from earlier, which shows not only delegation from an object (aka "instance") `a1` to object `Foo.prototype`, but from `Bar.prototype` to `Foo.prototype`, which somewhat resembles the concept of parent-child class inheritance. *Resembles*, except of course for the direction of the arrows, which show these are delegation links rather than copy operations.

And, here's the typical "prototype-style" code that creates such links:

```
function Foo(name) {
    this.name = name;
}

Foo.prototype.myName = function() {
    return this.name;
};

function Bar(name,label) {
    Foo.call( this, name );
    this.label = label;
}

// here, we make a new `Bar.prototype`
// linked to `Foo.prototype`
Bar.prototype = Object.create( Foo.prototype );

// Beware! Now `Bar.prototype.constructor` is gone,
// and might need to be manually "fixed" if you're
// in the habit of relying on such properties!

Bar.prototype.myLabel = function() {
    return this.label;
};

var a = new Bar( "a", "obj a" );

a.myName(); // "a"
a.myLabel(); // "obj a"
```

 To understand why this points to a in the previous code snippet, see Chapter 2.

The important part is `Bar.prototype = Object.create( Foo.prototype )`. The call to `Object.create(..)` *creates* a "new" object out of thin air, and links that new object's internal `[[Prototype]]` to the object you specify (`Foo.prototype` in this case).

In other words, that line says: "make a *new Bar dot prototype* object that's linked to *Foo dot prototype*."

When `function Bar() { .. }` is declared, `Bar`, like any other function, has a `.prototype` link to its default object. But *that* object is not linked to `Foo.prototype` like we want. So, we create a *new* object that *is* linked as we want, effectively throwing away the original incorrectly linked object.

A common misconception here is that either of the following approaches would *also* work, but they do not work as you'd expect:

```
// doesn't work like you want!
Bar.prototype = Foo.prototype;

// works kinda like you want, but with
// side effects you probably don't want :(
Bar.prototype = new Foo();
```

`Bar.prototype = Foo.prototype` doesn't create a new object for `Bar.prototype` to be linked to. It just makes `Bar.prototype` another reference to `Foo.prototype`, which effectively links `Bar` directly to the same object to which `Foo` links: `Foo.prototype`. This means when you start assigning, like `Bar.prototype.myLabel = ...`, you're modifying not a separate object but the shared `Foo.prototype` object itself, which would affect any objects linked to `Foo.prototype`. This is almost certainly not what you want. If it *is* what you want, then you likely don't need `Bar` at all, and should just use only `Foo` and make your code simpler.

`Bar.prototype = new Foo()` does in fact create a new object that is duly linked to `Foo.prototype` as we'd want. But, it used the `Foo(..)` "constructor call" to do it. If that function has any side effects (such as logging, changing state, registering against other objects, adding data properties to `this`, etc.), those side effects happen at the time of this linking (and likely against the wrong object!), rather than only when the eventual `Bar()` "descendents" are created, as would likely be expected.

So, we're left with using `Object.create(..)` to make a new object that's properly linked, but without having the side effects of calling `Foo(..)`. The slight downside is that we have to create a new object, throwing the old one away, instead of modifying the existing default object we're provided.

It would be *nice* if there was a standard and reliable way to modify the linkage of an existing object. Prior to ES6, there's a nonstandard and not fully cross-browser way, via the `.__proto__` property, which is settable. ES6 adds a `Object.setPrototypeOf(..)` helper utility, which does the trick in a standard and predictable way.

Compare the pre-ES6 and ES6-standardized techniques for linking `Bar.prototype` to `Foo.prototype`, side by side:

```
// pre-ES6
// throws away default existing `Bar.prototype`
Bar.prototype = Object.create( Foo.prototype );

// ES6+
// modifies existing `Bar.prototype`
Object.setPrototypeOf( Bar.prototype, Foo.prototype );
```

Ignoring the slight performance disadvantage (throwing away an object that's later garbage-collected) of the `Object.create(..)` approach, it's a little bit shorter and may be perhaps a little easier to read than the ES6+ approach. But it's probably a syntactic wash either way.

Inspecting "Class" Relationships

What if you have an object like `a` and want to find out what object (if any) it delegates to? Inspecting an instance (just an object in JS) for its inheritance ancestry (delegation linkage in JS) is often called *introspection* (or *reflection*) in traditional class-oriented environments.

Consider:

```
function Foo() {
    // ...
}

Foo.prototype.blah = ...;

var a = new Foo();
```

How do we then introspect `a` to find out its "ancestry" (delegation linkage)? The first approach embraces the "class" confusion:

```
a instanceof Foo; // true
```

The `instanceof` operator takes a plain object as its lefthand operand and a function as its righthand operand. The question `instanceof` answers is: in the entire `[[Prototype]]` chain of `a`, does the object arbitrarily pointed to by `Foo.prototype` ever appear?

Unfortunately, this means that you can only inquire about the "ancestry" of some object (`a`) if you have some function (`Foo`, with its attached `.prototype` reference) to test with. If you have two arbitrary objects, say `a` and `b`, and want to find out if *the objects* are related to each other through a [[Prototype]] chain, instanceof alone can't help.

 If you use the built-in .bind(..) utility to make a hard-bound function (see Chapter 2), the function created will not have a .prototype property. Using instanceof with such a function transparently substitutes the .prototype of the *target function* that the hard-bound function was created from.

It's fairly uncommon to use hard-bound functions as "constructor calls", but if you do, it will behave as if the original *target function* was invoked instead, which means that using instanceof with a hard-bound function also behaves according to the original function.

This snippet illustrates the ridiculousness of trying to reason about relationships between two objects using "class" semantics and instanceof:

```
// helper utility to see if `o1` is
// related to (delegates to) `o2`
function isRelatedTo(o1, o2) {
    function F(){}
    F.prototype = o2;
    return o1 instanceof F;
}

var a = {};
var b = Object.create( a );

isRelatedTo( b, a ); // true
```

Inside isRelatedTo(..), we borrow a throwaway function F, reassign its .prototype to arbitrarily point to some object o2, and then ask if o1 is an "instance of" F. Obviously o1 wasn't *actually* inherited or descended or even constructed from F, so it should be clear why this kind of exercise is silly and confusing. The problem comes down to the awkwardness of class semantics forced upon JavaScript, in this case as revealed by the indirect semantics of instanceof.

The second, and much cleaner, approach to [[Prototype]] reflection is:

```
Foo.prototype.isPrototypeOf( a ); // true
```

Notice that in this case, we don't really care (or even *need*) Foo, we just need an object (in our case, arbitrarily labeled Foo.prototype) to test against another object. The question `isPrototypeOf(..)` answers is: in the entire `[[Prototype]]` chain of `a`, does `Foo.prototype` ever appear?

Same question, and exact same answer. But in this second approach, we don't actually need the indirection of referencing a function (`Foo`) whose `.prototype` property will automatically be consulted.

We just need two objects to inspect a relationship between them. For example:

```
// Simply: does b appear anywhere in
// c's [[Prototype]] chain?
b.isPrototypeOf( c );
```

Notice that this approach doesn't require a function ("class") at all. It just uses object references directly to `b` and `c`, and inquires about their relationship. In other words, our `isRelatedTo(..)` utility is built in to the language, and it's called `isPrototypeOf(..)`.

We can also directly retrieve the `[[Prototype]]` of an object. As of ES5, the standard way to do this is:

```
Object.getPrototypeOf( a );
```

And you'll notice that object reference is what we'd expect:

```
Object.getPrototypeOf( a ) === Foo.prototype; // true
```

Most browsers (not all!) have also long supported a nonstandard alternate way of accessing the internal `[[Prototype]]`:

```
a.__proto__ === Foo.prototype; // true
```

The strange `.__proto__` (not standardized until ES6!) property "magically" retrieves the internal `[[Prototype]]` of an object as a reference, which is quite helpful if you want to directly inspect (or even traverse: `.__proto__.__proto__...`) the chain.

Just as we saw earlier with `.constructor`, `.__proto__` doesn't actually exist on the object you're inspecting (`a` in our running example). In fact, it exists (nonenumerable; see Chapter 2) on the built-in `Object.prototype`, along with the other common utilities (`.to String()`, `.isPrototypeOf(..)`, etc.).

Moreover, `.__proto__` looks like a property, but it's actually more appropriate to think of it as a getter/setter (see Chapter 3).

Roughly, we could envision .__proto__ implemented (see Chapter 3 for object property definitions) like this:

```
Object.defineProperty( Object.prototype, "__proto__", {
    get: function() {
        return Object.getPrototypeOf( this );
    },
    set: function(o) {
        // setPrototypeOf(..) as of ES6
        Object.setPrototypeOf( this, o );
        return o;
    }
} );
```

So, when we access (retrieve the value of) a.__proto__, it's like calling a.__proto__() (calling the getter function). *That* function call has a as its this even though the getter function exists on the Object.pro totype object (see Chapter 2 for this binding rules), so it's just like saying Object.getPrototypeOf(a).

.__proto__ is also a settable property, just like using ES6's Object.set PrototypeOf(..) shown earlier. However, generally you should not change the [[Prototype]] of an existing object.

There are some very complex, advanced techniques used deep in some frameworks that allow tricks like "subclassing" an Array, but this is commonly frowned on in general programming practice, as it usually leads to *much* harder to understand/maintain code.

 As of ES6, the class keyword will allow something that approximates "subclassing" of built-ins like Array. See Appendix A for discussion of the class syntax added in ES6.

The only other narrow exception (as mentioned earlier) would be setting the [[Prototype]] of a default function's .prototype object to reference some other object (besides Object.prototype). That would avoid replacing that default object entirely with a new linked object. Otherwise, it's best to treat object [[Prototype]] linkage as a read-only characteristic for ease of reading your code later.

The JavaScript community unofficially coined a term for the double underscore, specifically the leading one in properties like __proto__: "dunder." So, the "cool kids" in JavaScript would generally pronounce __proto__ as "dunder proto."

Object Links

As we've now seen, the [[Prototype]] mechanism is an internal link that exists on one object that references some other object.

This linkage is (primarily) exercised when a property/method reference is made against the first object, and no such property/method exists. In that case, the [[Prototype]] linkage tells the engine to look for the property/method on the linked-to object. In turn, if that object cannot fulfill the lookup, its [[Prototype]] is followed, and so on. This series of links between objects forms what is called the "prototype chain."

Create()ing Links

We've thoroughly debunked why JavaScript's [[Prototype]] mechanism is not like classes, and we've seen how it instead creates links between proper objects.

What's the point of the [[Prototype]] mechanism? Why is it so common for JS developers to go to so much effort (emulating classes) in their code to wire up these linkages?

Remember we said much earlier in this chapter that Object.create(..) would be a hero? Now, we're ready to see how:

```
var foo = {
    something: function() {
        console.log( "Tell me something good..." );
    }
};

var bar = Object.create( foo );

bar.something(); // Tell me something good...
```

Object.create(..) creates a new object (bar) linked to the object we specified (foo), which gives us all the power (delegation) of the [[Prototype]] mechanism, but without any of the unnecessary complication of new functions acting as classes and constructor calls, confusing `.prototype` and `.constructor` references, or any of that extra stuff.

 `Object.create(null)` creates an object that has an empty (aka null) `[[Prototype]]` linkage, and thus the object can't delegate anywhere. Since such an object has no prototype chain, the `instanceof` operator (explained earlier) has nothing to check, so it will always return `false`. These special empty-`[[Prototype]]` objects are often called "dictionaries," as they are typically used purely for storing data in properties, mostly because they have no possible surprise effects from any delegated properties/functions on the `[[Prototype]]` chain, and are thus purely flat data storage.

We don't *need* classes to create meaningful relationships between two objects. The only thing we should really care about is objects linked together for delegation, and `Object.create(..)` gives us that linkage without all the class cruft.

Object.create() polyfill

`Object.create(..)` was added in ES5. You may need to support pre-ES5 environments (like older IEs), so let's take a look at a simple *partial* polyfill for `Object.create(..)` that gives us the capability that we need even in those older JS environments:

```
if (!Object.create) {
    Object.create = function(o) {
        function F(){}
        F.prototype = o;
        return new F();
    };
}
```

This polyfill works by using a throwaway F function, and we override its `.prototype` property to point to the object we want to link to. Then we use `new F()` construction to make a new object that will be linked as we specified.

This usage of `Object.create(..)` is by far the most common usage, because it's the part that *can be* polyfilled. There's an additional set of functionality that the standard ES5 built-in `Object.create(..)` provides, which is *not polyfillable* for pre-ES5. As such, this capability is far less commonly used. For completeness sake, let's look at that additional functionality:

```
var anotherObject = {
    a: 2
};

var myObject = Object.create( anotherObject, {
    b: {
        enumerable: false,
        writable: true,
        configurable: false,
        value: 3
    },
    c: {
        enumerable: true,
        writable: false,
        configurable: false,
        value: 4
    }
} );

myObject.hasOwnProperty( "a" ); // false
myObject.hasOwnProperty( "b" ); // true
myObject.hasOwnProperty( "c" ); // true

myObject.a; // 2
myObject.b; // 3
myObject.c; // 4
```

The second argument to `Object.create(..)` specifies property names to add to the newly created object, via declaring each new property's *property descriptor* (see Chapter 3). Because polyfilling property descriptors into pre-ES5 is not possible, this additional functionality on `Object.create(..)` cannot be polyfilled.

The vast majority of usage of `Object.create(..)` uses the polyfill-safe subset of functionality, so most developers are fine with using the partial polyfill in pre-ES5 environments.

Some developers take a much stricter view, which is that no function should be polyfilled unless it can be *fully* polyfilled. Since `Object.create(..)` is one of those partial polyfillable utilities, this narrower perspective says that if you need to use any of the functionality of `Object.create(..)` in a pre-ES5 environment, instead of polyfilling, you should use a custom utility, and stay away from using the name `Object.create` entirely. You could instead define your own utility, like:

```
function createAndLinkObject(o) {
    function F(){}
    F.prototype = o;
    return new F();
}

var anotherObject = {
    a: 2
};

var myObject = createAndLinkObject( anotherObject );

myObject.a; // 2
```

I do not share this strict opinion. I fully endorse the common partial polyfill of `Object.create(..)` as shown earlier, and using it in your code even in pre-ES5. I'll leave it to you to make your own decision.

Links as Fallbacks?

It may be tempting to think that these links between objects *primarily* provide a sort of fallback for "missing" properties or methods. While that may be an observed outcome, I don't think it represents the right way of thinking about [[Prototype]].

Consider:

```
var anotherObject = {
    cool: function() {
        console.log( "cool!" );
    }
};

var myObject = Object.create( anotherObject );

myObject.cool(); // "cool!"
```

That code will work by virtue of [[Prototype]], but if you wrote it that way so that `anotherObject` was acting as a fallback just in case `myObject` couldn't handle some property/method that some developer may try to call, odds are that your software is going to be a bit more "magical" and harder to understand and maintain.

That's not to say there aren't cases where fallbacks are an appropriate design pattern, but it's not very common or idiomatic in JS, so if you find yourself doing so, you might want to take a step back and reconsider if that's really appropriate and sensible design.

In ES6, an advanced functionality called `Proxy` is introduced that can provide something of a "method not found" type of behavior. `Proxy` is beyond the scope of this book, but will be covered in detail in a later book in this series.

Don't miss an important but nuanced point here.

Designing software where you intend for a developer to, for instance, call `myObject.cool()` and have that work even though there is no `cool()` method on `myObject`, introduces some "magic" into your API design that can be surprising for future developers who maintain your software.

You can however design your API with less "magic" to it, but still take advantage of the power of `[[Prototype]]` linkage:

```
var anotherObject = {
    cool: function() {
        console.log( "cool!" );
    }
};

var myObject = Object.create( anotherObject );

myObject.doCool = function() {
    this.cool(); // internal delegation!
};

myObject.doCool(); // "cool!"
```

Here, we call `myObject.doCool()`, which is a method that *actually exists* on `myObject`, making our API design more explicit (less "magical"). *Internally*, our implementation follows the *delegation design pattern* (see Chapter 6), taking advantage of `[[Prototype]]` delegation to `anotherObject.cool()`.

In other words, delegation will tend to be less surprising/confusing if it's an internal implementation detail rather than plainly exposed in your API interface design. We will expound on delegation in great detail in the next chapter.

Review

When attempting a property access on an object that doesn't have that property, the object's internal `[[Prototype]]` linkage defines where the [[Get]] operation (see Chapter 3) should look next. This cascading linkage from object to object essentially defines a "prototype chain" (somewhat similar to a nested scope chain) of objects to traverse for property resolution.

All normal objects have the built-in Object.prototype as the top of the prototype chain (like the global scope in scope lookup), where property resolution will stop if not found anywhere prior in the chain. toString(), valueOf(), and several other common utilities exist on this Object.prototype object, explaining how all objects in the language are able to access them.

The most common way to get two objects linked to each other is using the new keyword with a function call, which among its four steps (see Chapter 2) creates a new object linked to another object.

The "another object" that the new object is linked to happens to be the object referenced by the arbitrarily named .prototype property of the function called with new. Functions called with new are often called "constructors," despite the fact that they are not actually instantiating a class as *constructors* do in traditional class-oriented languages.

While these JavaScript mechanisms can seem to resemble "class instantiation" and "class inheritance" from traditional class-oriented languages, the key distinction is that in JavaScript, no copies are made. Rather, objects end up linked to each other via an internal [[Prototype]] chain.

For a variety of reasons, not the least of which is terminology precedent, "inheritance" (and "prototypal inheritance") and all the other OO terms just do not make sense when considering how JavaScript *actually* works (not just applied to our forced mental models).

Instead, "delegation" is a more appropriate term, because these relationships are not *copies* but delegation links.

CHAPTER 6

Behavior Delegation

In Chapter 5, we addressed the `[[Prototype]]` mechanism in detail, and *why* it's confusing and inappropriate (despite countless attempts for nearly two decades) to describe it in the context of "class" or "inheritance." We trudged through not only the fairly verbose syntax (`.prototype` littering the code), but the various gotchas (like surprising `.constructor` resolution or ugly pseudopolymorphic syntax). We explored variations of the "mixin" approach, which many people use to attempt to smooth over such rough areas.

It's a common reaction at this point to wonder why it has to be so complex to do something seemingly so simple. Now that we've pulled back the curtain and seen just how dirty it all gets, it's not a surprise that most JS developers never dive this deep, and instead relegate such mess to a "class" library to handle it for them.

I hope by now you're not content to just gloss over and leave such details to a "black box" library. Let's now dig into how we *could and should be* thinking about the object `[[Prototype]]` mechanism in JS, in a *much simpler and more straightforward way* than the confusion of classes.

As a brief review of our conclusions from Chapter 5, the `[[Prototype]]` mechanism is an internal link that exists on one object that references another object.

This linkage is exercised when a property/method reference is made against the first object, and no such property/method exists. In that case, the `[[Prototype]]` linkage tells the engine to look for the property/method on the linked-to object. In turn, if that object cannot fulfill the lookup, its [[Prototype]] is followed, and so on. This series of links between objects forms what is called the "prototype chain."

In other words, the actual mechanism, the essence of what's important to the functionality we can leverage in JavaScript, is **all about objects being linked to other objects**.

That single observation is fundamental and critical to understanding the motivations and approaches for the rest of this chapter!

Toward Delegation-Oriented Design

To properly focus our thoughts on how to use [[Prototype]] in the most straightforward way, we must recognize that it represents a fundamentally different design pattern from classes (see Chapter 4).

 Some principles of class-oriented design are still very valid, so don't toss out everything you know (just most of it!). For example, *encapsulation* is quite powerful, and is compatible (though not as common) with delegation.

We need to try to change our thinking from the class/inheritance design pattern to the behavior delegation design pattern. If you have done most or all of your programming in your education/career thinking in classes, this may be uncomfortable or feel unnatural. You may need to try this mental exercise quite a few times to get the hang of this very different way of thinking.

I'm going to walk you through some theoretical exercises first, then we'll look side by side at a more concrete example to give you practical context for your own code.

Class Theory

Let's say we have several similar tasks ("XYZ," "ABC," etc.) that we need to model in our software.

With classes, the way you design the scenario is as follows: define a general parent (base) class like Task, defining shared behavior for all the "alike" tasks. Then, you define child classes XYZ and ABC, both of which inherit from Task, and each of which adds specialized behavior to handle its respective task.

Importantly, the class design pattern encourages you to employ method overriding (and polymorphism) to get the most out of inheritance, where you override the definition of some general `Task` method in your XYZ task, perhaps even making use of `super` to call to the base version of that method while adding more behavior to it. You'll likely find quite a few places where you can "abstract" out general behavior to the parent class and specialize (override) it in your child classes.

Here's some loose pseudocode for that scenario:

```
class Task {
    id;

    // constructor `Task()`
    Task(ID) { id = ID; }
    outputTask() { output( id ); }
}

class XYZ inherits Task {
    label;

    // constructor `XYZ()`
    XYZ(ID,Label) { super( ID ); label = Label; }
    outputTask() { super(); output( label ); }
}

class ABC inherits Task {
    // ...
}
```

Now, you can instantiate one or more *copies* of the XYZ child class, and use those instance(s) to perform task "XYZ." These instances have copies both of the general `Task` defined behavior as well as the specific XYZ defined behavior. Likewise, instances of the ABC class would have copies of the `Task` behavior and the specific ABC behavior. After construction, you will generally only interact with these instances (and not the classes), as the instances each have copies of all the behavior you need to do the intended task.

Delegation Theory

But now let's try to think about the same problem domain, using *behavior delegation* instead of *classes*.

You will first define an *object* (not a class, nor a `function` as most JSers would lead you to believe) called `Task`, and it will have concrete behavior on it that includes utility methods that various tasks can use (read: *delegate to!*). Then, for each task ("XYZ," "ABC"), you define an object to hold that task-specific data/behavior. You *link* your task-specific object(s) to the Task utility object, allowing them to delegate to it when they need to.

Basically, think about needing behaviors from two sibling/peer objects (XYZ and Task) to perform task "XYZ." But rather than needing to compose them together, via class copies, we can keep them in their separate objects, and we can allow the XYZ object to delegate to Task when needed.

Here's some simple code to suggest how you accomplish that:

```
Task = {
    setID: function(ID) { this.id = ID; },
    outputID: function() { console.log( this.id ); }
};

// make `XYZ` delegate to `Task`
XYZ = Object.create( Task );

XYZ.prepareTask = function(ID,Label) {
    this.setID( ID );
    this.label = Label;
};

XYZ.outputTaskDetails = function() {
    this.outputID();
    console.log( this.label );
};

// ABC = Object.create( Task );
// ABC ... = ...
```

In this code, Task and XYZ are not classes (or functions), they're just objects. XYZ is set up via Object.create(..) to [[Prototype]]-delegate to the Task object (see Chapter 5).

As compared to class orientation (aka object orientation), **I call this style of code OLOO (objects linked to other objects)**. All we *really* care about is that the XYZ object delegates to the Task object (as does the ABC object).

In JavaScript, the [[Prototype]] mechanism links objects to other objects. There are no abstract mechanisms like "classes," no matter how much you try to convince yourself otherwise. It's like paddling a canoe upstream: you *can* do it, but you're *choosing* to go against the natural current, so it's obviously going to be harder to get where you're going.

Some other differences to note with OLOO-style code:

1. Both the `id` and `label` data members from the previous class example are data properties directly on XYZ (neither is on Task). In general, with [[Prototype]] delegation, you want state to be on the delegators (XYZ, ABC), not on the delegate (Task).

2. With the class design pattern, we intentionally named `output Task` the same on both parent (Task) and child (XYZ), so that we could take advantage of overriding (polymorphism). In behavior delegation, we do the opposite: we avoid if at all possible naming things the same at different levels of the [[Prototype]] chain (called shadowing—see Chapter 5), because having those name collisions creates awkward/brittle syntax to disambiguate references (see Chapter 4), and we want to avoid that if we can.

   This design pattern calls for less use of general method names that are prone to overriding and instead more use of descriptive method names, *specific* to the type of behavior each object is doing. This can actually create easier to understand/maintain code, because the names of methods (not only at the definition location but strewn throughout other code) are more obvious (self-documenting).

3. `this.setID(ID);` inside of a method on the XYZ object first looks on XYZ for `setID(..)`, but since it doesn't find a method of that name on XYZ, [[Prototype]] *delegation* means it can follow the link to Task to look for `setID(..)`, which it of course finds. Moreover, because of implicit call-site `this` binding rules (see Chapter 2), when `setID(..)` runs, even though the method was found on Task, the `this` binding for that function call is XYZ, exactly as we'd expect and want. We see the same thing with `this.outpu tID()` later in the code listing.

   In other words, the general utility methods that exist on Task are available to us while interacting with XYZ, because XYZ can delegate to Task.

Behavior delegation means to let some object (XYZ) provide a delegation (to Task) for property or method references if they are not found on the object (XYZ).

This is an *extremely powerful* design pattern, very distinct from the ideas of parent and child classes, inheritance, polymorphism, etc. Rather than organizing the objects in your mind vertically, with parents flowing down to children, think of objects side by side, as peers, with any direction of delegation links between the objects as necessary.

 Delegation is more properly used as an internal implementation detail rather than exposed directly in the API interface design. In the previous example, we don't necessarily *intend* with our API design for developers to call XYZ.setID() (though we can, of course!). We sorta *hide* the delegation as an internal detail of our API, where XYZ.prepareTask(..) delegates to Task.setID(..). See "Links as Fallbacks?" on page 110 in Chapter 5 for more detail.

Mutual delegation (disallowed)

You cannot create a *cycle* where two or more objects are mutually delegated (bidirectionally) to each other. If you link B to A, and then try to link A to B, you will get an error.

It's a shame (not terribly surprising, but mildly annoying) that this is disallowed. If you made a reference to a property/method that didn't exist in either place, you'd have an infinite recursion on the [[Prototype]] loop. But if all references were strictly present, then B could delegate to A, and vice versa, and it *could* work. This would mean you could use either object to delegate to the other, for various tasks. There are a few niche use cases where this might be helpful.

But it's disallowed because engine implementors have observed that it's more performant to check for (and reject!) the infinite circular reference once at set-time rather than needing to have the performance hit of that guard check every time you look up a property on an object.

Debugged

We'll briefly cover a subtle detail that can be confusing to developers. In general, the JS specification does not control how browser developer tools should represent specific values/structures to a developer, so each browser/engine is free to interpret such things as it sees fit. As such, browsers/tools *don't always agree*. Specifically, the behavior we will now examine is currently observed only in Chrome's Developer Tools.

Consider this traditional "class constructor" style JS code, as it would appear in the *console* of Chrome Developer Tools:

```
function Foo() {}

var a1 = new Foo();

a1; // Foo {}
```

Let's look at the last line of that snippet: the output of evaluating the a1 expression, which prints Foo {}. If you try this same code in Firefox, you will likely see Object {}. Why the difference? What do these outputs mean?

Chrome is essentially saying "{} is an empty object that was constructed by a function with name *Foo*." Firefox is saying "{} is an empty object of general construction from *Object*." The subtle difference is that Chrome is actively tracking, as an *internal property*, the name of the actual function that did the construction, whereas other browsers don't track that additional information.

It would be tempting to attempt to explain this with JavaScript mechanisms:

```
function Foo() {}

var a1 = new Foo();

a1.constructor; // Foo(){}
a1.constructor.name; // "Foo"
```

So, is that how Chrome is outputting Foo, by simply examining the object's .constructor.name? Confusingly, the answer is both yes and no.

Consider this code:

```
function Foo() {}

var a1 = new Foo();

Foo.prototype.constructor = function Gotcha(){};

a1.constructor; // Gotcha(){}
a1.constructor.name; // "Gotcha"

a1; // Foo {}
```

Even though we change a1.constructor.name to legitimately be something else (Gotcha), Chrome's console still uses the Foo name.

So, it would appear the answer to previous question (does it use `.con` `structor.name`?) is *no*; it must track it somewhere else, internally.

But not so fast! Let's see how this kind of behavior works with OLOO-style code:

```
var Foo = {};

var a1 = Object.create( Foo );

a1; // Object {}

Object.defineProperty( Foo, "constructor", {
    enumerable: false,
    value: function Gotcha(){}
});

a1; // Gotcha {}
```

Ah-ha! Gotcha! Here, Chrome's console *did* find and use the `.con` `structor.name`. Actually, while writing this book, this exact behavior was identified as a bug in Chrome, and by the time you're reading this, it may have already been fixed. So you may instead have seen the corrected `a1; // Object {}`.

Aside from that bug, the internal tracking (apparently only for debug output purposes) of the "constructor name" that Chrome does (shown in the earlier snippets) is an intentional Chrome-only extension of behavior beyond what the JS specification calls for.

If you don't use a "constructor" to make your objects, as we've discouraged with OLOO-style code here in this chapter, then you'll get objects that Chrome does *not* track an internal "constructor name" for, and such objects will correctly only be outputted as `Object {}`, meaning "object generated from Object() construction."

Don't think this represents a drawback of OLOO-style coding. When you code with OLOO and behavior delegation as your design pattern, *who* "constructed" (that is, *which function* was called with `new`?) some object is an irrelevant detail. Chrome's specific internal "constructor name" tracking is really only useful if you're fully embracing class-style coding, but is moot if you're instead embracing OLOO delegation.

Mental Models Compared

Now that you can see a difference between "class" and "delegation" design patterns, at least theoretically, let's see the implications these design patterns have on the mental models we use to reason about our code.

We'll examine some more theoretical (Foo, Bar) code, and compare both ways (OO versus OLOO) of implementing the code. The first snippet uses the classical ("prototypal") OO style:

```
function Foo(who) {
    this.me = who;
}
Foo.prototype.identify = function() {
    return "I am " + this.me;
};

function Bar(who) {
    Foo.call( this, who );
}
Bar.prototype = Object.create( Foo.prototype );

Bar.prototype.speak = function() {
    alert( "Hello, " + this.identify() + "." );
};

var b1 = new Bar( "b1" );
var b2 = new Bar( "b2" );

b1.speak();
b2.speak();
```

Parent class Foo is inherited by child class Bar, which is then instantiated twice as b1 and b2. What we have is b1 delegating to Bar.prototype, which delegates to Foo.prototype. This should look fairly familiar to you, at this point. Nothing too groundbreaking going on.

Now, let's implement *the exact same functionality* using OLOO-style code:

```
Foo = {
    init: function(who) {
        this.me = who;
    },
    identify: function() {
        return "I am " + this.me;
    }
```

```
};

Bar = Object.create( Foo );

Bar.speak = function() {
    alert( "Hello, " + this.identify() + "." );
};

var b1 = Object.create( Bar );
b1.init( "b1" );
var b2 = Object.create( Bar );
b2.init( "b2" );

b1.speak();
b2.speak();
```

We take exactly the same advantage of [[Prototype]] delegation from b1 to Bar to Foo as we did in the previous snippet between b1, Bar.pro totype, and Foo.prototype. *We still have the same three objects linked together.*

But, importantly, we've greatly simplified all the other stuff going on, because now we just set up objects linked to each other, without needing all the cruft and confusion of things that look (but don't behave!) like classes, with constructors and prototypes and new calls.

Ask yourself: if I can get the same functionality with OLOO-style code as I do with class-style code, but OLOO is simpler and has less things to think about, isn't OLOO better?

Let's examine the mental models involved between these two snippets.

First, the class-style code snippet implies this mental model of entities and their relationships:

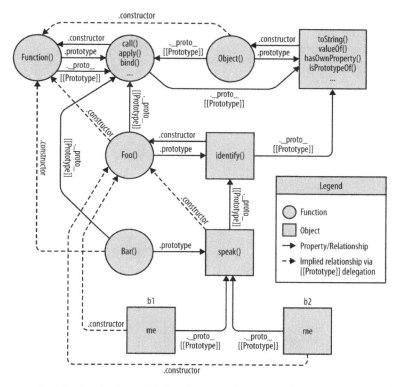

Actually, that's a little unfair/misleading, because it's showing a lot of extra detail that you don't *technically* need to know at all times (though you *do* need to understand it!). One takeaway is that it's quite a complex series of relationships. But another takeaway: if you spend the time to follow those relationship arrows around, there's an amazing amount of internal consistency in JS's mechanisms.

For instance, the ability of a JS function to access call(..), ap ply(..), and bind(..) (see Chapter 2) is because functions themselves are objects, and function-objects also have a [[Prototype]] linkage, to the Function.prototype object, which defines those default methods that any function-object can delegate to. JS can do those things, *and you can too!*

OK, let's now look at a *slightly* simplified version of that diagram that is a little more "fair" for comparison—it shows only the *relevant* entities and relationships:

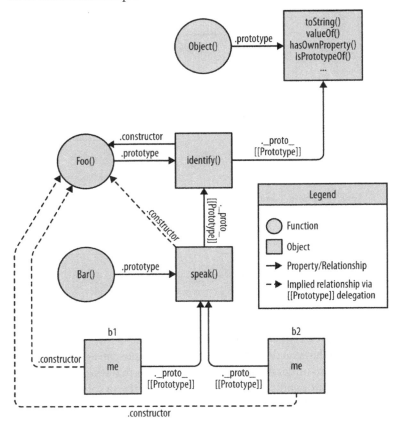

Still pretty complex, eh? The dotted lines are depicting the implied relationships when you set up the "inheritance" between `Foo.proto type` and `Bar.prototype` and haven't yet *fixed* the missing `.construc tor` property reference (see ""Constructor" redux" on page 98 in Chapter 5). Even with those dotted lines removed, the mental model is still an awful lot to juggle every time you work with object linkages.

Now, let's look at the mental model for OLOO-style code:

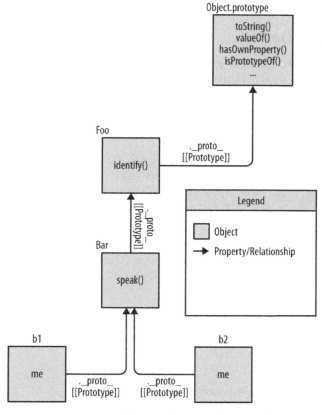

As you can see comparing them, it's quite obvious that OLOO-style code has vastly less stuff to worry about, because OLOO-style code embraces the fact that the only thing we ever really cared about was the *objects linked to other objects*.

All the other "class" cruft was a confusing and complex way of getting the same end result. Remove that stuff, and things get much simpler (without losing any capability).

Classes Versus Objects

We've just seen various theoretical explorations and mental models of "classes" versus "behavior delegation." But, let's now look at more concrete code scenarios to show how'd you actually use these ideas.

We'll first examine a typical scenario in frontend web dev: creating UI widgets (buttons, drop-downs, etc.).

Widget "Classes"

Because you're probably still so used to the OO design pattern, you'll likely immediately think of this problem domain in terms of a parent class (perhaps called `Widget`) with all the common base widget behavior, and then child derived classes for specific widget types (like `Button`).

 We're going to use jQuery here for DOM and CSS manipulation, only because it's a detail we don't really care about for the purposes of our current discussion. None of this code cares which JS framework (jQuery, Dojo, YUI, etc.), if any, you might solve such mundane tasks with.

Let's examine how we'd implement the "class" design in classic-style pure JS without any "class" helper library or syntax:

```
// Parent class
function Widget(width,height) {
    this.width = width || 50;
    this.height = height || 50;
    this.$elem = null;
}

Widget.prototype.render = function($where){
    if (this.$elem) {
        this.$elem.css( {
            width: this.width + "px",
            height: this.height + "px"
        } ).appendTo( $where );
    }
};

// Child class
function Button(width,height,label) {
    // "super" constructor call
    Widget.call( this, width, height );
    this.label = label || "Default";

    this.$elem = $( "<button>" ).text( this.label );
}

// make `Button` "inherit" from `Widget`
Button.prototype = Object.create( Widget.prototype );
```

```
// override base "inherited" `render(..)`
Button.prototype.render = function($where) {
    // "super" call
    Widget.prototype.render.call( this, $where );
    this.$elem.click( this.onClick.bind( this ) );
};

Button.prototype.onClick = function(evt) {
    console.log( "Button '" + this.label + "' clicked!" );
};

$( document ).ready( function(){
    var $body = $( document.body );
    var btn1 = new Button( 125, 30, "Hello" );
    var btn2 = new Button( 150, 40, "World" );

    btn1.render( $body );
    btn2.render( $body );
} );
```

OO design patterns tell us to declare a base render(..) in the parent class, then override it in our child class, not to replace it per se, but rather to augment the base functionality with button-specific behavior.

Notice the ugliness of explicit pseudopolymorphism (see Chapter 4) with Widget.call and Widget.prototype.render.call references for faking "super" calls from the child "class" methods back up to the "parent" class base methods. Yuck.

ES6 class sugar

We cover ES6 class syntax sugar in detail in Appendix A, but let's briefly demonstrate how we'd implement the same code using class:

```
class Widget {
    constructor(width,height) {
        this.width = width || 50;
        this.height = height || 50;
        this.$elem = null;
    }
    render($where){
        if (this.$elem) {
            this.$elem.css( {
                width: this.width + "px",
                height: this.height + "px"
            } ).appendTo( $where );
        }
    }
}
```

```
class Button extends Widget {
    constructor(width,height,label) {
        super( width, height );
        this.label = label || "Default";
        this.$elem = $( "<button>" ).text( this.label );
    }
    render($where) {
        super( $where );
        this.$elem.click( this.onClick.bind( this ) );
    }
    onClick(evt) {
        console.log( "Button '" + this.label + "' clicked!" );
    }
}

$( document ).ready( function(){
    var $body = $( document.body );
    var btn1 = new Button( 125, 30, "Hello" );
    var btn2 = new Button( 150, 40, "World" );

    btn1.render( $body );
    btn2.render( $body );
} );
```

Undoubtedly, a number of the syntax uglies of the previous classical approach have been smoothed over with ES6's class. The presence of a super(..) in particular seems quite nice (though when you dig into it, it's not all roses!).

Despite syntactic improvements, these are not *real* classes, as they still operate on top of the [[Prototype]] mechanism. They suffer from all the same mental-model mismatches we explored in Chapters 4 and 5 and thus far in this chapter. Appendix A will expound on the ES6 class syntax and its implications in detail. We'll see why solving syntax hiccups doesn't substantially solve our class confusions in JS, though it makes a valiant effort masquerading as a solution!

Whether you use the classic prototypal syntax or the new ES6 sugar, you've still made a *choice* to model the problem domain (UI widgets) with "classes." And as the previous few chapters try to demonstrate, this *choice* in JavaScript is opting you into extra headaches and mental tax.

Delegating Widget Objects

Here's our simpler `Widget`/`Button` example, using OLOO-style delegation:

```
var Widget = {
    init: function(width,height){
        this.width = width || 50;
        this.height = height || 50;
        this.$elem = null;
    },
    insert: function($where){
        if (this.$elem) {
            this.$elem.css( {
                width: this.width + "px",
                height: this.height + "px"
            } ).appendTo( $where );
        }
    }
};

var Button = Object.create( Widget );

Button.setup = function(width,height,label){
    // delegated call
    this.init( width, height );
    this.label = label || "Default";

    this.$elem = $( "<button>" ).text( this.label );
};
Button.build = function($where) {
    // delegated call
    this.insert( $where );
    this.$elem.click( this.onClick.bind( this ) );
};
Button.onClick = function(evt) {
    console.log( "Button '" + this.label + "' clicked!" );
};

$( document ).ready( function(){
    var $body = $( document.body );

    var btn1 = Object.create( Button );
    btn1.setup( 125, 30, "Hello" );

    var btn2 = Object.create( Button );
    btn2.setup( 150, 40, "World" );

    btn1.build( $body );
    btn2.build( $body );
} );
```

With this OLOO-style approach, we don't think of `Widget` as a parent and `Button` as a child. Rather, `Widget` is just an object and is sort of a utility collection that any specific type of widget might want to delegate to, and `Button` is also just a standalone object (with a delegation link to `Widget`, of course!).

From a design pattern perspective, we didn't share the same method name `render(..)` in both objects, the way classes suggest, but instead we chose different names (`insert(..)` and `build(..)`) that were more descriptive of what task each does specifically. The *initialization* methods are called `init(..)` and `setup(..)`, respectively, for the same reasons.

Not only does this delegation design pattern suggest different and more descriptive names (rather than shared and more generic names), but doing so with OLOO happens to avoid the ugliness of the explicit pseudopolymorphic calls (`Widget.call` and `Widget.prototype.ren der.call`), as you can see by the simple, relative, delegated calls to `this.init(..)` and `this.insert(..)`.

Syntactically, we also don't have any constructors, `.prototype`, or `new` present, as they are, in fact, just unnecessary cruft.

Now, if you're paying close attention, you may notice that what was previously just one call (`var btn1 = new Button(..)`) is now two calls (`var btn1 = Object.create(Button)` and `btn1.setup(..)`). Initially this may seem like a drawback (more code).

However, even this is something that's a pro of OLOO-style code as compared to classical prototype style code. How?

With class constructors, you are forced (not really, but it is strongly suggested) to do both construction and initialization in the same step. However, there are many cases where being able to do these two steps separately (as you do with OLOO!) is more flexible.

For example, let's say you create all your instances in a pool at the beginning of your program, but you wait to initialize them with a specific setup when they are pulled from the pool and used. We showed the two calls happening right next to each other, but of course they can happen at very different times and in very different parts of our code, as needed.

OLOO better supports the principle of separation of concerns, where creation and initialization are not necessarily conflated into the same operation.

Simpler Design

In addition to OLOO providing ostensibly simpler (and more flexible!) code, behavior delegation as a pattern can actually lead to simpler code architecture. Let's examine one last example that illustrates how OLOO simplifies your overall design.

The scenario we'll examine is two controller objects, one for handling the login form of a web page, and another for actually handling the authentication (communication) with the server.

We'll need a utility helper for making the Ajax communication to the server. We'll use jQuery (though any framework would do fine), since it handles not only the Ajax for us, but it returns a Promise-like answer so that we can listen for the response in our calling code with `.then(..)`.

 We don't cover Promises here, but we will cover them in a future title of this series.

Following the typical class design pattern, we'll put the base functionality of the task in a class called `Controller`, and then we'll derive two child classes, `LoginController` and `AuthController`, which both inherit from `Controller` and specialize some of those base behaviors:

```
// Parent class
function Controller() {
    this.errors = [];
}
Controller.prototype.showDialog(title,msg) {
    // display title & message to user in dialog
};
Controller.prototype.success = function(msg) {
    this.showDialog( "Success", msg );
};
Controller.prototype.failure = function(err) {
    this.errors.push( err );
    this.showDialog( "Error", err );
};
```

```
// Child class
function LoginController() {
    Controller.call( this );
}
// Link child class to parent
LoginController.prototype =
    Object.create( Controller.prototype );
LoginController.prototype.getUser = function() {
    return document.getElementById( "login_username" ).value;
};
LoginController.prototype.getPassword = function() {
    return document.getElementById( "login_password" ).value;
};
LoginController.prototype.validateEntry = function(user,pw) {
    user = user || this.getUser();
    pw = pw || this.getPassword();

    if (!(user && pw)) {
        return this.failure(
            "Please enter a username & password!"
        );
    }
    else if (user.length < 5) {
        return this.failure(
            "Password must be 5+ characters!"
        );
    }

    // got here? validated!
    return true;
};
// Override to extend base `failure()`
LoginController.prototype.failure = function(err) {
    // "super" call
    Controller.prototype.failure.call(
        this,
        "Login invalid: " + err
    );
};

// Child class
function AuthController(login) {
    Controller.call( this );
    // in addition to inheritance, we also need composition
    this.login = login;
}
// Link child class to parent
AuthController.prototype =
    Object.create( Controller.prototype );
AuthController.prototype.server = function(url,data) {
    return $.ajax( {
```

```
            url: url,
            data: data
        } );
};
AuthController.prototype.checkAuth = function() {
    var user = this.login.getUser();
    var pw = this.login.getPassword();

    if (this.login.validateEntry( user, pw )) {
        this.server( "/check-auth",{
            user: user,
            pw: pw
        } )
        .then( this.success.bind( this ) )
        .fail( this.failure.bind( this ) );
    }
};
// Override to extend base `success()`
AuthController.prototype.success = function() {
    // "super" call
    Controller.prototype.success.call( this, "Authenticated!" );
};
// Override to extend base `failure()`
AuthController.prototype.failure = function(err) {
    // "super" call
    Controller.prototype.failure.call(
        this,
        "Auth Failed: " + err
    );
};

var auth = new AuthController();
auth.checkAuth(
    // in addition to inheritance, we also need composition
    new LoginController()
);
```

We have base behaviors that all controllers share, which are suc
cess(..), failure(..), and showDialog(..). Our child classes Log
inController and AuthController override failure(..) and suc
cess(..) to augment the default base class behavior. Also note that
AuthController needs an instance of LoginController to interact
with the login form, so that becomes a member data property.

The other thing to mention is that we chose some *composition* to
sprinkle in on top of the inheritance. AuthController needs to know
about LoginController, so we instantiate it (new LoginControl
ler()) and keep a class member property called this.login to

reference it, so that `AuthController` can invoke behavior on `Logi nController`.

There *might* have been a slight temptation to make `AuthCon troller` inherit from `LoginController`, or vice versa, such that we had *virtual composition* through the inheritance chain. But this is a clear example of what's wrong with class inheritance as *the* model for the problem domain, because neither `AuthController` nor `LoginController` are specializing base behavior of the other, so inheritance between them makes little sense except if classes are your only design pattern. Instead, we layered in some simple *composition* and now they can cooperate, while still both benefiting from the inheritance from the parent base `Controller`.

If you're familiar with class-oriented (OO) design, this should all look pretty familiar and natural.

De-class-ified

But, do we really need to model this problem with a parent `Control ler` class, two child classes, and some composition? Is there a way to take advantage of OLOO-style behavior delegation and have a *much* simpler design? Yes!

```
var LoginController = {
    errors: [],
    getUser: function() {
        return document.getElementById(
            "login_username"
        ).value;
    },
    getPassword: function() {
        return document.getElementById(
            "login_password"
        ).value;
    },
    validateEntry: function(user,pw) {
        user = user || this.getUser();
        pw = pw || this.getPassword();

        if (!(user && pw)) {
            return this.failure(
                "Please enter a username & password!"
            );
        }
```

```
            else if (user.length < 5) {
                return this.failure(
                    "Password must be 5+ characters!"
                );
            }

            // got here? validated!
            return true;
        },
        showDialog: function(title,msg) {
            // display success message to user in dialog
        },
        failure: function(err) {
            this.errors.push( err );
            this.showDialog( "Error", "Login invalid: " + err );
        }
    };

    // Link `AuthController` to delegate to `LoginController`
    var AuthController = Object.create( LoginController );

    AuthController.errors = [];
    AuthController.checkAuth = function() {
        var user = this.getUser();
        var pw = this.getPassword();

        if (this.validateEntry( user, pw )) {
            this.server( "/check-auth",{
                user: user,
                pw: pw
            } )
            .then( this.accepted.bind( this ) )
            .fail( this.rejected.bind( this ) );
        }
    };
    AuthController.server = function(url,data) {
        return $.ajax( {
            url: url,
            data: data
        } );
    };
    AuthController.accepted = function() {
        this.showDialog( "Success", "Authenticated!" )
    };
    AuthController.rejected = function(err) {
        this.failure( "Auth Failed: " + err );
    };
```

Since AuthController is just an object (so is LoginController), we don't need to instantiate (like new AuthController()) to perform our task. All we need to do is:

```
AuthController.checkAuth();
```

Of course, with OLOO, if you do need to create one or more additional objects in the delegation chain, that's easy, and still doesn't require anything like class instantiation:

```
var controller1 = Object.create( AuthController );
var controller2 = Object.create( AuthController );
```

With behavior delegation, `AuthController` and `LoginController` are just objects, *horizontal* peers of each other, and are not arranged or related as parents and children in class orientation. We somewhat arbitrarily chose to have `AuthController` delegate to `LoginController`; it would have been just as valid for the delegation to go the reverse direction.

The main takeaway from this second code listing is that we only have two entities (`LoginController` and `AuthController`), not three as before.

We didn't need a base `Controller` class to "share" behavior between the two, because delegation is a powerful enough mechanism to give us the functionality we need. We also, as noted before, don't need to instantiate our classes to work with them, because there are no classes, just the objects themselves. Furthermore, there's no need for *composition*, as delegation gives the two objects the ability to cooperate *differentially* as needed.

Lastly, we avoided the polymorphism pitfalls of class-oriented design by not having the names `success(..)` and `failure(..)` be the same on both objects, which would have required ugly explicit pseudopolymorphism. Instead, we called them `accepted()` and `rejected(..)` on `AuthController`—slightly more descriptive names for their specific tasks.

Bottom line: we end up with the same capability, but a (significantly) simpler design. That's the power of OLOO-style code and the power of the *behavior delegation* design pattern.

Nicer Syntax

One of the nicer things that makes ES6's `class` so deceptively attractive (see Appendix A on why to avoid it!) is the shorthand syntax for declaring class methods:

```
class Foo {
    methodName() { /* .. */ }
}
```

We get to drop the word `function` from the declaration, which makes JS developers everywhere cheer!

And you may have noticed and been frustrated that the previously suggested OLOO syntax has lots of `function` appearances, which seems like a bit of a detractor to the goal of OLOO simplification. But it doesn't have to be that way!

As of ES6, we can use *concise method declarations* in any object literal, so an object in OLOO style can be declared this way (same shorthand sugar as with the `class` body syntax):

```
var LoginController = {
    errors: [],
    getUser() { // Look ma, no `function`!
        // ...
    },
    getPassword() {
        // ...
    }
    // ...
};
```

About the only difference is that object literals will still require , comma separators between elements whereas `class` syntax doesn't. Pretty minor concession in the whole scheme of things.

Moreover, as of ES6, the clunkier syntax you use (like for the `AuthCon troller` definition), where you're assigning properties individually and not using an object literal, can be rewritten using an object literal (so that you can use concise methods), and you can just modify that object's `[[Prototype]]` with `Object.setPrototypeOf(..)`, like this:

```
// use nicer object literal syntax w/ concise methods!
var AuthController = {
    errors: [],
    checkAuth() {
        // ...
    },
    server(url,data) {
        // ...
    }
    // ...
};
```

```
// NOW, link `AuthController` to delegate to `LoginController`
Object.setPrototypeOf( AuthController, LoginController );
```

OLOO style as of ES6, with concise methods, is a lot friendlier than it was before (and even then, it was much simpler and nicer than classical prototype-style code). You don't have to opt for class (complexity) to get nice clean object syntax!

Unlexical

There *is* one drawback to concise methods that's subtle but important to note. Consider this code:

```
var Foo = {
    bar() { /*..*/ },
    baz: function baz() { /*..*/ }
};
```

Here's the syntactic de-sugaring that expresses how that code will operate:

```
var Foo = {
    bar: function() { /*..*/ },
    baz: function baz() { /*..*/ }
};
```

See the difference? The bar() shorthand became an *anonymous function expression* (function()..) attached to the bar property, because the function object itself has no name identifier. Compare that to the manually specified *named function expression* (function baz()..), which has a lexical name identifier baz in addition to being attached to a .baz property.

So what? In the *Scope & Closures* title of this book series, we cover the three main downsides of *anonymous function expressions* in detail. We'll just briefly repeat them so we can compare to the concise method shorthand.

The lack of a name identifier on an anonymous function:

1. Makes debugging stack traces harder

2. Makes self-referencing (recursion, event (un)binding, etc.) harder

3. Makes code (a little bit) harder to understand

Items 1 and 3 don't apply to concise methods.

Even though the de-sugaring uses an *anonymous function expression,* which normally would have no name in stack traces, concise methods are specified to set the internal name property of the function object accordingly, so stack traces should be able to use it (though that's implementation dependent so not guaranteed).

Item 2 is, unfortunately, still a drawback to concise methods. They will not have a lexical identifier to use as a self-reference. Consider:

```
var Foo = {
    bar: function(x) {
        if (x < 10) {
            return Foo.bar( x * 2 );
        }
        return x;
    },
    baz: function baz(x) {
        if (x < 10) {
            return baz( x * 2 );
        }
        return x;
    }
};
```

The manual Foo.bar(x*2) reference kind of suffices in this example, but there are many cases where a function wouldn't necessarily be able to do that, such as cases where the function is being shared in delegation across different objects, using this binding, etc. You would want to use a real self-reference, and the function object's name identifier is the best way to accomplish that.

Just be aware of this caveat for concise methods, and if you run into such issues with lack of self-reference, make sure to forego the concise method syntax *just for that declaration* in favor of the manual *named function expression* declaration form: baz: function baz(){..}.

Introspection

If you've spent much time with class-oriented programming (either in JS or other languages), you're probably familiar with *type introspection*: inspecting an instance to find out what *kind* of object it is. The primary goal of *type introspection* with class instances is to reason about the structure/capabilities of the object based on *how it was created.*

Consider this code that uses `instanceof` (see Chapter 5) for intro-specting on an object `a1` to infer its capability:

```
function Foo() {
    // ...
}
Foo.prototype.something = function(){
    // ...
}

var a1 = new Foo();

// later

if (a1 instanceof Foo) {
    a1.something();
}
```

Because `Foo.prototype` (not Foo!) is in the `[[Prototype]]` chain (see Chapter 5) of `a1`, the `instanceof` operator (confusingly) pretends to tell us that `a1` is an instance of the Foo "class." With this knowledge, we then assume that `a1` has the capabilities described by the Foo "class."

Of course, there is no Foo class, only a plain old normal function Foo, which happens to have a reference to an arbitrary object (`Foo.prototype`) that `a1` happens to be delegation-linked to. By its syntax, `instanceof` pretends to be inspecting the relationship between `a1` and Foo, but it's actually telling us whether `a1` and (the arbitrary object referenced by) `Foo.prototype` are related.

The semantic confusion (and indirection) of `instanceof` syntax means that to use `instanceof`-based introspection to ask if object `a1` is related to the capabilities object in question, you *have to* have a function that holds a reference to that object—you can't just directly ask if the two objects are related.

Recall the abstract `Foo/Bar/b1` example from earlier in this chapter, which we'll abbreviate here:

```
function Foo() { /* .. */ }
Foo.prototype...

function Bar() { /* .. */ }
Bar.prototype = Object.create( Foo.prototype );

var b1 = new Bar( "b1" );
```

For type introspection purposes on the entities in that example, using `instanceof` and `.prototype` semantics, here are the various checks you might need to perform:

```
// relating `Foo` and `Bar` to each other
Bar.prototype instanceof Foo; // true
Object.getPrototypeOf( Bar.prototype )
    === Foo.prototype; // true
Foo.prototype.isPrototypeOf( Bar.prototype ); // true

// relating `b1` to both `Foo` and `Bar`
b1 instanceof Foo; // true
b1 instanceof Bar; // true
Object.getPrototypeOf( b1 ) === Bar.prototype; // true
Foo.prototype.isPrototypeOf( b1 ); // true
Bar.prototype.isPrototypeOf( b1 ); // true
```

It's fair to say that some of that kinda sucks. For instance, intuitively (with classes) you might want to be able to say something like `Bar instanceof Foo` (because it's easy to mix up what "instance" means to think it includes "inheritance"), but that's not a sensible comparison in JS. You have to do `Bar.prototype instanceof Foo` instead.

Another common, but perhaps less robust, pattern for type introspection, which many devs seem to prefer over `instanceof`, is called "duck typing." This term comes from the adage, "if it looks like a duck, and it quacks like a duck, it must be a duck."

Example:

```
if (a1.something) {
    a1.something();
}
```

Rather than inspecting for a relationship between `a1` and an object that holds the delegatable `something()` function, we assume that the test for `a1.something` passing means `a1` has the capability to call `.something()` (regardless of if it found the method directly on `a1` or delegated to some other object). In and of itself, that assumption isn't so risky.

But "duck typing" is often extended to make other assumptions about the object's capabilities besides what's being tested, which of course introduces more risk (aka brittle design) into the test.

One notable example of "duck typing" comes with ES6 Promises (which as an earlier note explained, are not being covered in this book).

For various reasons, there's a need to determine if any arbitrary object reference *is a Promise*, but the way that test is done is to check if the object happens to have a then() function present on it. In other words, if any object happens to have a then() method, ES6 Promises will assume unconditionally that the object is a "thenable" and therefore will expect it to behave conformantly to all standard behaviors of Promises.

If you have any non-Promise object that happens for whatever reason to have a then() method on it, you are strongly advised to keep it far away from the ES6 Promise mechanism to avoid broken assumptions.

That example clearly illustrates the perils of "duck typing." You should only use such approaches sparingly and in controlled conditions.

Turning our attention once again back to OLOO-style code as presented here in this chapter, type introspection turns out to be much cleaner. Let's recall (and abbreviate) the Foo/Bar/b1 OLOO example from earlier in the chapter:

```
var Foo = { /* .. */ };

var Bar = Object.create( Foo );
Bar...

var b1 = Object.create( Bar );
```

Using this OLOO approach, where all we have are plain objects that are related via [[Prototype]] delegation, here's the quite simplified type introspection we might use:

```
// relating `Foo` and `Bar` to each other
Foo.isPrototypeOf( Bar ); // true
Object.getPrototypeOf( Bar ) === Foo; // true

// relating `b1` to both `Foo` and `Bar`
Foo.isPrototypeOf( b1 ); // true
Bar.isPrototypeOf( b1 ); // true
Object.getPrototypeOf( b1 ) === Bar; // true
```

We're not using instanceof anymore, because it's confusingly pretending to have something to do with classes. Now, we just ask the (informally stated) question, "Are you *a* prototype of me?" There's no more indirection necessary with stuff like Foo.prototype or the painfully verbose Foo.prototype.isPrototypeOf(..).

I think it's fair to say these checks are significantly less complicated/confusing that the previous set of introspection checks. Yet again, we see that OLOO is simpler than (but with all the same power of) class-style coding in JavaScript.

Review

Classes and inheritance are a design pattern you can *choose*, or *not choose*, in your software architecture. Most developers take for granted that classes are the only (proper) way to organize code, but here we've seen there's another less-commonly talked about pattern that's actually quite powerful: *behavior delegation*.

Behavior delegation suggests objects as peers of each other, which delegate among themselves, rather than parent and child class relationships. JavaScript's [[Prototype]] mechanism is, by its very designed nature, a behavior delegation mechanism. That means we can either choose to struggle to implement class mechanics on top of JS (see Chapters 4 and 5), or we can just embrace the natural state of [[Prototype]] as a delegation mechanism.

When you design code with objects only, not only does it simplify the syntax you use, but it can actually lead to simpler code architecture design.

OLOO (objects linked to other objects) is a code style that creates and relates objects directly without the abstraction of classes. OLOO quite naturally implements [[Prototype]]-based behavior delegation.

ES6 Class

If there's any takeaway message from the second half of this book (Chapters 4-6), it's that classes are an optional design pattern for code (not a necessary given), and that furthermore they are often quite awkward to implement in a [[Prototype]] language like JavaScript.

This awkwardness is *not* just about syntax, although that's a big part of it. Chapters 4 and 5 examined quite a bit of syntactic ugliness, from the verbosity of .prototype references cluttering the code, to *explicit pseudo-polymorphism* (see Chapter 4) when you give methods the same name at different levels of the chain and try to implement a polymorphic reference from a lower-level method to a higher-level method. .constructor being wrongly interpreted as "was constructed by" and yet being unreliable for that definition is yet another syntactic ugly.

But the problems with class design are much deeper. Chapter 4 points out that classes in traditional class-oriented languages actually produce a *copy* action from parent to child to instance, whereas in [[Prototype]], the action is not a copy, but rather the opposite—a delegation link.

When compared to the simplicity of OLOO-style code and behavior delegation (see Chapter 6), which embrace [[Prototype]] rather than hide from it, classes stand out as a sore thumb in JS.

class

But we *don't* need to argue that case again. I remention those issues briefly only so that you keep them fresh in your mind now that we turn our attention to the ES6 `class` mechanism. We'll demonstrate here how it works, and look at whether or not `class` does anything substantial to address any of those "class" concerns.

Let's revisit the `Widget`/`Button` example from Chapter 6:

```
class Widget {
    constructor(width,height) {
        this.width = width || 50;
        this.height = height || 50;
        this.$elem = null;
    }
    render($where){
        if (this.$elem) {
            this.$elem.css( {
                width: this.width + "px",
                height: this.height + "px"
            } ).appendTo( $where );
        }
    }
}

class Button extends Widget {
    constructor(width,height,label) {
        super( width, height );
        this.label = label || "Default";
        this.$elem = $( "<button>" ).text( this.label );
    }
    render($where) {
        super( $where );
        this.$elem.click( this.onClick.bind( this ) );
    }
    onClick(evt) {
        console.log( "Button '" + this.label + "' clicked!" );
    }
}
```

Beyond this syntax *looking* nicer, what problems does ES6 solve?

1. There's no more (well, sorta, see below!) references to `.proto type` cluttering the code.

2. `Button` is declared directly to "inherit from" (aka `extends`) `Widg et`, instead of needing to use `Object.create(..)` to replace

a `.prototype` object that's linked, or having to set with `.__pro to__` or `Object.setPrototypeOf(..)`.

3. `super(..)` now gives us a very helpful relative polymorphism capability, so that any method at one level of the chain can refer relatively one level up the chain to a method of the same name. This includes a solution to the note from Chapter 4 about the weirdness of constructors not belonging to their class, and so being unrelated—`super()` works inside constructors exactly as you'd expect.

4. `class` literal syntax has no affordance for specifying properties (only methods). This might seem limiting to some, but it's expected that the vast majority of cases where a property (state) exists elsewhere but the end-chain "instances" is usually a mistake and surprising (as it's state that's implicitly "shared" among all "instances"). So, one *could* say the `class` syntax is protecting you from mistakes.

5. `extends` lets you extend even built-in object (sub)types, like `Ar ray` or `RegExp`, in a very natural way. Doing so without `class ..` `extends` has long been an exceedingly complex and frustrating task, one that only the most adept of framework authors have ever been able to accurately tackle. Now, it will be rather trivial!

In all fairness, those are some substantial solutions to many of the most obvious (syntactic) issues and surprises people have with classical prototype-style code.

class Gotchas

It's not all bubblegum and roses, though. There are still some deep and profoundly troubling issues with using "classes" as a design pattern in JS.

First, the `class` syntax may convince you a new "class" mechanism exists in JS as of ES6. Not so. `class` is, mostly, just syntactic sugar on top of the existing `[[Prototype]]` (delegation!) mechanism.

That means `class` is not actually copying definitions statically at declaration time the way it does in traditional class-oriented languages. If you change/replace a method (on purpose or by accident) on the parent "class," the child "class" and/or instances will still be affected, in that they don't get copies at declaration time; they are all still using the live-delegation model based on [[Prototype]]:

```
class C {
    constructor() {
        this.num = Math.random();
    }
    rand() {
        console.log( "Random: " + this.num );
    }
}

var c1 = new C();
c1.rand(); // "Random: 0.4324299..."

C.prototype.rand = function() {
    console.log( "Random: " + Math.round( this.num * 1000 ));
};

var c2 = new C();
c2.rand(); // "Random: 867"

c1.rand(); // "Random: 432" -- oops!!!
```

This only seems like reasonable behavior *if you already know* about the delegation nature of things, rather than expecting *copies* from "real classes." So the question to ask yourself is, why are you choosing class syntax for something fundamentally different from classes?

Doesn't the ES6 class syntax just make it harder to see and understand the difference between traditional classes and delegated objects?

class syntax *does not* provide a way to declare class member properties (only methods). So if you need to do that to track shared state among instances, then you end up going back to the ugly .proto type syntax, like this:

```
class C {
    constructor() {
        // make sure to modify the shared state,
        // not set a shadowed property on the
        // instances!
        C.prototype.count++;

        // here, `this.count` works as expected
        // via delegation
        console.log( "Hello: " + this.count );
    }
}
```

```
// add a property for shared state directly to
// prototype object
C.prototype.count = 0;

var c1 = new C();
// Hello: 1

var c2 = new C();
// Hello: 2

c1.count === 2; // true
c1.count === c2.count; // true
```

The biggest problem here is that it betrays the class syntax by exposing (leakage!) .prototype as an implementation detail.

But, we also still have the surprise gotcha that this.count++ would implicitly create a separate shadowed .count property on both the c1 and c2 objects, rather than updating the shared state. class offers us no consolation from that issue, except (presumably) to imply by lack of syntactic support that you shouldn't be doing that *at all*.

Moreover, accidental shadowing is still a hazard:

```
class C {
    constructor(id) {
        // oops, gotcha, we're shadowing `id()` method
        // with a property value on the instance
        this.id = id;
    }
    id() {
        console.log( "Id: " + id );
    }
}

var c1 = new C( "c1" );
c1.id(); // TypeError -- `c1.id` is now the string "c1"
```

There's also some very subtle nuanced issues with how super works. You might assume that super would be bound in an analogous way to how this gets bound (see Chapter 2), which is that super would always be bound to one level higher than whatever the current method's position in the [[Prototype]] chain is.

However, for performance reasons (this binding is already expensive), super is not bound dynamically. It's bound sort of "statically" at declaration time. No big deal, right?

Ehh...maybe, maybe not. If you, like most JS devs, start assigning functions around to different objects (which came from class definitions), in various different ways, you probably won't be very aware that in all those cases, the super mechanism under the covers is having to be rebound each time.

And depending on what sorts of syntactic approaches you take to these assignments, there may very well be cases where the super can't be properly bound (at least, not where you suspect), so you may (at the time of writing, TC39 discussion is ongoing on the topic) have to manually bind super with toMethod(..) (kinda like you have to do bind(..) for this—see Chapter 2).

You're used to being able to assign around methods to different objects to *automatically* take advantage of the dynamicism of this via the *implicit binding* rule (see Chapter 2). But the same will likely not be true with methods that use super.

Consider what super should do here (against D and E):

```
class P {
    foo() { console.log( "P.foo" ); }
}

class C extends P {
    foo() {
        super();
    }
}

var c1 = new C();
c1.foo(); // "P.foo"

var D = {
    foo: function() { console.log( "D.foo" ); }
};

var E = {
    foo: C.prototype.foo
};

// Link E to D for delegation
Object.setPrototypeOf( E, D );

E.foo(); // "P.foo"
```

If you were thinking (quite reasonably!) that super would be bound dynamically at call time, you might expect that super() would automatically recognize that E delegates to D, so E.foo() using super() should call to D.foo().

Not so. For performance pragmatism reasons, super is not *late bound* (aka dynamically bound) like this is. Instead it's derived at call time from [[HomeObject]].[[Prototype]], where [[HomeObject]] is statically bound at creation time.

In this particular case, super() is still resolving to P.foo(), since the method's [[HomeObject]] is still C and C.[[Prototype]] is P.

There will *probably* be ways to manually address such gotchas. Using toMethod(..) to bind/rebind a method's [[HomeObject]] (along with setting the [[Prototype]] of that object!) appears to work in this scenario:

```
var D = {
    foo: function() { console.log( "D.foo" ); }
};

// Link E to D for delegation
var E = Object.create( D );

// manually bind foo's `[[HomeObject]]` as
// `E`, and `E.[[Prototype]]` is `D`, so thus
// `super()` is `D.foo()`
E.foo = C.prototype.foo.toMethod( E, "foo" );

E.foo(); // "D.foo"
```

 toMethod(..) clones the method and takes homeObject as its first parameter (which is why we pass E), and the second parameter (optionally) sets a name for the new method (which we keep as "foo").

It remains to be seen if there are other corner case gotchas that devs will run into beyond this scenario. Regardless, you will have to be diligent and stay aware of which places the engine automatically figures out super for you, and which places you have to manually take care of it. Ugh!

Static > Dynamic?

But the biggest problem of all for the ES6 `class` is that all these various gotchas mean `class` sorta opts you into a syntax that seems to imply (like traditional classes) that once you declare a `class`, it's a static definition of a (future instantiated) thing. You completely lose sight of the fact C is an object, a concrete thing, which you can directly interact with.

In traditional class-oriented languages, you never adjust the definition of a class later, so the class design pattern doesn't suggest such capabilities. But one of the most powerful parts of JS is that it *is* dynamic, and the definition of any object is (unless you make it immutable) a fluid and mutable *thing*.

`class` seems to imply you shouldn't do such things, by forcing you into the uglier `.prototype` syntax to do so, or forcing you think about `super` gotchas, etc. It also offers *very little* support for any of the pitfalls that this dynamicism can bring.

In other words, it's as if `class` is telling you: "Dynamic is too hard, so it's probably not a good idea. Here's a static-looking syntax, so code your stuff statically."

What a sad commentary on JavaScript: *dynamic is too hard, let's pretend to be (but not actually be!) static.*

These are the reasons why the ES6 `class` is masquerading as a nice solution to syntactic headaches, but it's actually muddying the waters further and making things worse for JS and for clear and concise understanding.

 If you use the `.bind(..)` utility to make a hard-bound function (see Chapter 2), the function created is not subclassable with ES6 `extend` like normal functions are.

Review

`class` does a very good job of pretending to fix the problems with the class/inheritance design pattern in JS. But it actually does the opposite: it hides many of the problems and introduces other subtle but dangerous ones.

`class` contributes to the ongoing confusion of "class" in JavaScript that has plagued the language for nearly two decades. In some respects, it asks more questions than it answers, and it feels like a very unnatural fit on top of the elegant simplicity of the `[[Prototype]]` mechanism.

Bottom line: if the ES6 `class` makes it harder to robustly leverage `[[Prototype]]`, and hides the most important nature of the JS object mechanism—the live delegation links between objects—shouldn't we see `class` as creating more troubles than it solves, and just relegate it to an antipattern?

I can't really answer that question for you. But I hope this book has fully explored the issue at a deeper level than you've ever gone before, and has given you the information you need *to answer it yourself.*

Acknowledgments

I have many people to thank for making this book and the overall series happen.

First, I must thank my wife, Christen Simpson, and my two kids, Ethan and Emily, for putting up with Dad always pecking away at the computer. Even when not writing books, my obsession with JavaScript glues my eyes to the screen far more than it should. That time I borrow from my family is the reason these books can so deeply and completely explain JavaScript to you, the reader. I owe my family everything.

I'd like to thank my editors at O'Reilly, namely Simon St.Laurent and Brian MacDonald, as well as the rest of the editorial and marketing staff. They are fantastic to work with, and have been especially accommodating during this experiment into "open source" book writing, editing, and production.

Thank you to the many folks who have participated in making this book series better by providing editorial suggestions and corrections, including Shelley Powers, Tim Ferro, Evan Borden, Forrest L Norvell, Jennifer Davis, Jesse Harlin, Nick Berardi, and many others.

Thank you to the countless folks in the community, including members of the TC39 committee, who have shared so much knowledge with the rest of us, and especially tolerated my incessant questions and explorations with patience and detail. John-David Dalton, Juriy "kangax" Zaytsev, Mathias Bynens, Rick Waldron, Axel Rauschmayer, Nicholas Zakas, Angus Croll, Jordan Harband, Reginald Braithwaite, Dave Herman, Brendan Eich, Allen Wirfs-Brock, Bradley Meck, Domenic Denicola, David Walsh, Tim Disney, Kris Kowal, Peter van der

Zee, Andrea Giammarchi, Kit Cambridge, and so many others, I can't even scratch the surface.

Since this book series was born on Kickstarter, I also wish to thank all my (nearly) 500 generous backers, without whom this book series could not have happened: Jan Szpila, nokiko, Murali Krishnamoorthy, Ryan Joy, Craig Patchett, pdqtrader, Dale Fukami, ray hatfield, R0drigo Perez [Mx], Dan Petitt, Jack Franklin, Andrew Berry, Brian Grinstead, Rob Sutherland, Sergi Meseguer, Phillip Gourley, Mark Watson, Jeff Carouth, Alfredo Sumaran, Martin Sachse, Marcio Barrios, Dan, AimelyneM, Matt Sullivan, Delnatte Pierre-Antoine, Jake Smith, Eugen Tudorancea, Iris, David Trinh, simonstl, Ray Daly, Uros Gruber, Justin Myers, Shai Zonis, Mom & Dad, Devin Clark, Dennis Palmer, Brian Panahi Johnson, Josh Marshall, Marshall, Dennis Kerr, Matt Steele, Erik Slagter, Sacah, Justin Rainbow, Christian Nilsson, Delapouite, D.Pereira, Nicolas Hoizey, George V. Reilly, Dan Reeves, Bruno Laturner, Chad Jennings, Shane King, Jeremiah Lee Cohick, od3n, Stan Yamane, Marko Vucinic, Jim B, Stephen Collins, Ægir Þorsteinsson, Eric Pederson, Owain, Nathan Smith, Jeanetteurphy, Alexandre ELISÉ, Chris Peterson, Rik Watson, Luke Matthews, Justin Lowery, Morten Nielsen, Vernon Kesner, Chetan Shenoy, Paul Tregoing, Marc Grabanski, Dion Almaer, Andrew Sullivan, Keith Elsass, Tom Burke, Brian Ashenfelter, David Stuart, Karl Swedberg, Graeme, Brandon Hays, John Christopher, Gior, manoj reddy, Chad Smith, Jared Harbour, Minoru TODA, Chris Wigley, Daniel Mee, Mike, Handyface, Alex Jahraus, Carl Furrow, Rob Foulkrod, Max Shishkin, Leigh Penny Jr., Robert Ferguson, Mike van Hoenselaar, Hasse Schougaard, rajan venkataguru, Jeff Adams, Trae Robbins, Rolf Langenhuijzen, Jorge Antunes, Alex Koloskov, Hugh Greenish, Tim Jones, Jose Ochoa, Michael Brennan-White, Naga Harish Muvva, Barkóczi Dávid, Kitt Hodsden, Paul McGraw, Sascha Goldhofer, Andrew Metcalf, Markus Krogh, Michael Mathews, Matt Jared, Juanfran, Georgie Kirschner, Kenny Lee, Ted Zhang, Amit Pahwa, Inbal Sinai, Dan Raine, Schabse Laks, Michael Tervoort, Alexandre Abreu, Alan Joseph Williams, NicolasD, Cindy Wong, Reg Braithwaite, LocalPCGuy, Jon Friskics, Chris Merriman, John Pena, Jacob Katz, Sue Lockwood, Magnus Johansson, Jeremy Crapsey, Grzegorz Pawłowski, nico nuzzaci, Christine Wilks, Hans Bergren, charles montgomery, Ariel בר-לבב Fogel, Ivan Kolev, Daniel Campos, Hugh Wood, Christian Bradford, Frédéric Harper, Ionuț Dan Popa, Jeff Trimble, Rupert Wood, Trey Carrico, Pancho Lopez, Joël kuijten, Tom A Marra, Jeff Jewiss, Jacob Rios, Paolo Di Stefano, Soledad Penades, Chris Gerber, Andrey Dolganov, Wil Moore

III, Thomas Martineau, Kareem, Ben Thouret, Udi Nir, Morgan Laupies, jory carson-burson, Nathan L Smith, Eric Damon Walters, Derry Lozano-Hoyland, Geoffrey Wiseman, mkeehner, KatieK, Scott MacFarlane, Brian LaShomb, Adrien Mas, christopher ross, Ian Littman, Dan Atkinson, Elliot Jobe, Nick Dozier, Peter Wooley, John Hoover, dan, Martin A. Jackson, Héctor Fernando Hurtado, andy ennamorato, Paul Seltmann, Melissa Gore, Dave Pollard, Jack Smith, Philip Da Silva, Guy Israeli, @megalithic, Damian Crawford, Felix Gliesche, April Carter Grant, Heidi, jim tierney, Andrea Giammarchi, Nico Vignola, Don Jones, Chris Hartjes, Alex Howes, john gibbon, David J. Groom, BBox, Yu *Dilys* Sun, Nate Steiner, Brandon Satrom, Brian Wyant, Wesley Hales, Ian Pouncey, Timothy Kevin Oxley, George Terezakis, sanjay raj, Jordan Harband, Marko McLion, Wolfgang Kaufmann, Pascal Peuckert, Dave Nugent, Markus Liebelt, Welling Guzman, Nick Cooley, Daniel Mesquita, Robert Syvarth, Chris Coyier, Rémy Bach, Adam Dougal, Alistair Duggin, David Loidolt, Ed Richer, Brian Chenault, GoldFire Studios, Carles Andrés, Carlos Cabo, Yuya Saito, roberto ricardo, Barnett Klane, Mike Moore, Kevin Marx, Justin Love, Joe Taylor, Paul Dijou, Michael Kohler, Rob Cassie, Mike Tierney, Cody Leroy Lindley, tofuji, Shimon Schwartz, Raymond, Luc De Brouwer, David Hayes, Rhys Brett-Bowen, Dmitry, Aziz Khoury, Dean, Scott Tolinski - Level Up, Clement Boirie, Djordje Lukic, Anton Kotenko, Rafael Corral, Philip Hurwitz, Jonathan Pidgeon, Jason Campbell, Joseph C., SwiftOne, Jan Hohner, Derick Bailey, getify, Daniel Cousineau, Chris Charlton, Eric Turner, David Turner, Joël Galeran, Dharma Vagabond, adam, Dirk van Bergen, dave ♥♫★ furf, Vedran Zakanj, Ryan McAllen, Natalie Patrice Tucker, Eric J. Bivona, Adam Spooner, Aaron Cavano, Kelly Packer, Eric J, Martin Drenovac, Emilis, Michael Pelikan, Scott F. Walter, Josh Freeman, Brandon Hudgeons, vijay chennupati, Bill Glennon, Robin R., Troy Forster, otaku_coder, Brad, Scott, Frederick Ostrander, Adam Brill, Seb Flippence, Michael Anderson, Jacob, Adam Randlett, Standard, Joshua Clanton, Sebastian Kouba, Chris Deck, SwordFire, Hannes Papenberg, Richard Woeber, hnzz, Rob Crowther, Jedidiah Broadbent, Sergey Chernyshev, Jay-Ar Jamon, Ben Combee, luciano bonachela, Mark Tomlinson, Kit Cambridge, Michael Melgares, Jacob Adams, Adrian Bruinhout, Bev Wieber, Scott Puleo, Thomas Herzog, April Leone, Daniel Mizieliński, Kees van Ginkel, Jon Abrams, Erwin Heiser, Avi Laviad, David newell, Jean-Francois Turcot, Niko Roberts, Erik Dana, Charles Neill, Aaron Holmes, Grzegorz Ziółkowski, Nathan Youngman, Timothy, Jacob Mather, Michael Allan, Mohit Seth, Ryan Ewing, Benjamin Van Treese,

Marcelo Santos, Denis Wolf, Phil Keys, Chris Yung, Timo Tijhof, Martin Lekvall, Agendine, Greg Whitworth, Helen Humphrey, Dougal Campbell, Johannes Harth, Bruno Girin, Brian Hough, Darren Newton, Craig McPheat, Olivier Tille, Dennis Roethig, Mathias Bynens, Brendan Stromberger, sundeep, John Meyer, Ron Male, John F Croston III, gigante, Carl Bergenhem, B.J. May, Rebekah Tyler, Ted Foxberry, Jordan Reese, Terry Suitor, afeliz, Tom Kiefer, Darragh Duffy, Kevin Vanderbeken, Andy Pearson, Simon Mac Donald, Abid Din, Chris Joel, Tomas Theunissen, David Dick, Paul Grock, Brandon Wood, John Weis, dgrebb, Nick Jenkins, Chuck Lane, Johnny Megahan, marzsman, Tatu Tamminen, Geoffrey Knauth, Alexander Tarmolov, Jeremy Tymes, Chad Auld, Sean Parmelee, Rob Staenke, Dan Bender, Yannick derwa, Joshua Jones, Geert Plaisier, Tom LeZotte, Christen Simpson, Stefan Bruvik, Justin Falcone, Carlos Santana, Michael Weiss, Pablo Villoslada, Peter deHaan, Dimitris Iliopoulos, seyDoggy, Adam Jordens, Noah Kantrowitz, Amol M, Matthew Winnard, Dirk Ginader, Phinam Bui, David Rapson, Andrew Baxter, Florian Bougel, Michael George, Alban Escalier, Daniel Sellers, Sasha Rudan, John Green, Robert Kowalski, David I. Teixeira (@ditma, Charles Carpenter, Justin Yost, Sam S, Denis Ciccale, Kevin Sheurs, Yannick Croissant, Pau Fracés, Stephen McGowan, Shawn Searcy, Chris Ruppel, Kevin Lamping, Jessica Campbell, Christopher Schmitt, Sablons, Jonathan Reisdorf, Bunni Gek, Teddy Huff, Michael Mullany, Michael Fürstenberg, Carl Henderson, Rick Yoesting, Scott Nichols, Hernán Ciudad, Andrew Maier, Mike Stapp, Jesse Shawl, Sérgio Lopes, jsulak, Shawn Price, Joel Clermont, Chris Ridmann, Sean Timm, Jason Finch, Aiden Montgomery, Elijah Manor, Derek Gathright, Jesse Harlin, Dillon Curry, Courtney Myers, Diego Cadenas, Arne de Bree, João Paulo Dubas, James Taylor, Philipp Kraeutli, Mihai Păun, Sam Gharegozlou, joshjs, Matt Murchison, Eric Windham, Timo Behrmann, Andrew Hall, joshua price, and Théophile Villard.

This book series is being written in open source, including editing and production. We owe GitHub a debt of gratitude for making that sort of thing possible for the community!

Thank you again to all the countless folks I didn't name but who I nonetheless owe thanks. May this book series be "owned" by all of us and serve to contribute to increasing awareness and understanding of the JavaScript language, to the benefit of all current and future community contributors.

About the Author

Kyle Simpson is an Open Web Evangelist from Austin, TX. He's passionate about JavaScript, HTML5, real-time/peer-to-peer communications, and web performance. Otherwise, he's probably bored by it. Kyle is an author, workshop trainer, tech speaker, and avid OSS community member.

Colophon

The cover font for *this & Object Prototypes* is Interstate. The text font is Adobe Minion Pro; the heading font is Adobe Myriad Condensed; and the code font is Dalton Maag's Ubuntu Mono.

Have it your way.

Get even more for your money.

Join the O'Reilly Community, and register the O'Reilly books you own. It's free, and you'll get:

- $4.99 ebook upgrade offer
- 40% upgrade offer on O'Reilly print books
- Membership discounts on books and events
- Free lifetime updates to ebooks and videos
- Multiple ebook formats, DRM FREE
- Participation in the O'Reilly community
- Newsletters
- Account management
- 100% Satisfaction Guarantee

Signing up is easy:

1. Go to: oreilly.com/go/register
2. Create an O'Reilly login.
3. Provide your address.
4. Register your books.

Note: English-language books only

To order books online:
oreilly.com/store

For questions about products or an order:
orders@oreilly.com

To sign up to get topic-specific email announcements and/or news about upcoming books, conferences, special offers, and new technologies:
elists@oreilly.com

For technical questions about book content:
booktech@oreilly.com

To submit new book proposals to our editors:
proposals@oreilly.com

O'Reilly books are available in multiple DRM-free ebook formats. For more information:
oreilly.com/ebooks

O'REILLY®

DISCARD

CPSIA information can be obtained at www.ICGtesting.com
Printed in the USA
BVOW08s0548140714

358959BV00003B/3/P